Crafting Your KICKASS Life's Masterpiece.

Mickey Trivett

Name of Book:
Live Life, Do Good, Be Happy! Crafting Your KICKASS Life's Masterpiece.

Author: *Mickey Trivett*
Publisher: *BeHappyBrands.com*

Copyright © 2023 Mickey Trivett. All rights reserved.

No part of this book may be reproduced in any form or by any electronic or mechanical means, including information storage and retrieval systems, without written permission from the author, except for the use of brief quotations in a book review.

Legal Disclaimer:

The information in this book is meant to educate and entertain. The author and publisher have made every effort to ensure the accuracy of the information herein. However, the information contained in this book is presented without warranty, either express or implied. The reader of this book assumes all responsibility for the use of these materials and information. The author assumes no responsibility or liability whatsoever on behalf of any reader of these materials.

All advice, opinions, and other materials in this book are those of Mickey Trivett. Each reader is responsible for making their own decisions and choices based on the advice, opinions, and materials provided. The author is not responsible for the consequences of any decisions or actions taken by the reader.

KICKASS Foreword

Listen up, you badass warrior! This is it—the moment you've been waiting for. The time has come to embark on the most KICKASS journey of your life, the epic adventure that will transform you from the inside out, setting your soul on fire and leaving you hungry for more. Are you ready to unleash your inner badass and live life on your terms? Hell yeah, you are!

This book isn't just another self-help guide; it's an unapologetic, in-your-face, no-holds-barred blueprint for living your most extraordinary life. It's time to stop playing small, to break free from the chains of societal norms and expectations, and to boldly step into your greatness. Your life's masterpiece is waiting to be crafted, and it all starts right here, right now.

As you flip through these pages, you'll dive headfirst into the art of living life on your terms, embracing your authentic self, and pursuing your passions with an unstoppable fire in your soul. You'll learn the power of saying "no" and setting boundaries, how to build and nurture KICKASS connections, and the thrill of embracing the unknown. This book is your guide to breaking free from the constraints of societal norms and expectations, boldly stepping into your greatness, and crafting the masterpiece that is your life.

You're about to uncover the keys to genuine happiness, fearlessly facing change, and daring to dream big. You'll be challenged to unleash your inner rebel, master the art of vulnerability, and practice mindfulness in every aspect of your life.

But this isn't just about inspiration and motivation—it's about action. You'll be armed with practical tools, strategies, and insights that will empower you to take charge of your life and make your dreams a reality. You'll explore the world of bulletproof confidence, the joy of discomfort, and the life-changing power of habits.
This KICKASS journey won't be a walk in the park—it's going to be tough, it's going to be raw, and it's going to push you to your limits. But I promise you this: the rewards will be worth it. You'll emerge from this experience a stronger, more resilient, and more fulfilled version of yourself.

So, take a deep breath, summon your courage, and get ready to dive in. Your best life is waiting for you on the other side of these pages. This is the book that will ignite the spark within you and set you on the path to living your most extraordinary life. Say goodbye to mediocrity and hello to a world where anything is possible.

Are you ready? Hell yes, you are! Let's do this.

KICKASS DEDICATION

To my incredible KICKASS dad, the rock-solid foundation of my life,

This book is fiercely and wholeheartedly dedicated to you. Your unwavering support, wisdom, and love have ignited a fire within me to chase what truly matters: happiness, experiences, and the relentless pursuit of a life lived to its fullest.

You've taught me the art of giving without expecting anything in return, of valuing relationships over material wealth, and of striving to be the best version of myself every damn day. It's because of you that I've discovered my passion, embraced my journey, and dared to dream bigger.

As I walk down this wild and unpredictable path called life, I'm eternally grateful for your guiding hand, your infectious optimism, and your unwavering belief in me. I hope to become half the man you are, and carry on your legacy of kindness, resilience, and boundless spirit.

With every page of this book, your love, lessons, and legacy shine through, inspiring not just me, but everyone who reads it to seize the day and follow their heart.

In gratitude and admiration, I dedicate this book to you, Dad, as a testament to the incredible impact you've had on my life and the world.

KICKASS Foreward (Page 3)

KICKASS Dedication (Page 5)

Table of Contents (Page 6)

Chapter 1: Embracing Your Badass Self
1. F*ck the Expectations: Why it's crucial to stop living life by other people's standards and start living for yourself. (Page 16)

2. The Art of Being Unapologetically You: How to embrace your true self and not give a damn about societal norms. (Page 18)

3. Powering Through Impostor Syndrome: Why you're more than enough and how to own your greatness. (Page 20)

4. The Confidence Catalyst: How building self-confidence can transform your life and help you conquer your fears. (Page 24)

Chapter 2: The Life-Changing Magic of Saying "No"
1. The 'No' Mindset: How saying no can open up more opportunities for growth and success. (Page 30)

2. Prioritize Like a Boss: Strategies for effectively managing your time and energy by saying no to what doesn't serve you. (Page 32)

3. The No-F*cks-Given Guide to Setting Boundaries: Protecting your peace of mind and establishing healthy personal boundaries. (Page 34)

4. The Rewards of Saying No: How embracing the power of rejection can unlock a world of freedom, self-respect, and personal growth. (Page 36)

Chapter 3: Building KICKASS Connections

1. The Science of Genuine Connection: Understanding the power of authentic relationships and their impact on happiness. (Page 40)

2. Networking for the Soul: How to create meaningful connections beyond superficial encounters. (Page 42)

3. Nurturing Your Tribe: Strategies for maintaining and strengthening your relationships with your inner circle. (Page 45)

4. Letting Go: Knowing when it's time to cut ties and move on from toxic or unfulfilling relationships. (Page 47)

Chapter 4: Embracing the Thrill of the Unknown

1. The Adventure Mindset: How to approach life with a sense of curiosity and excitement, making every day an adventure. (Page 52)

2. Jumping Off the Comfort Cliff: The benefits of taking risks and stepping out of your comfort zone. (Page 56)

3. The Art of Failing Forward: Learning from your failures and using them as stepping stones to success. (Page 59)

4. Living Life to the Fullest: Discovering true happiness through experiences, not material possessions, and embracing the present moment. (Page 661)

Chapter 5: The Pursuit of Genuine Happiness
1. Defining Happiness: Debunking myths about happiness and understanding what it truly means to be happy. (Page 66)

2. The Gratitude Attitude: Harnessing the power of gratitude to elevate your happiness levels. (Page 68)

3. The Ultimate Guide to Self-Care: Prioritizing mental, emotional, and physical well-being in the quest for happiness. (Page 71)

4. The Ripple Effect: How spreading positivity and kindness can create a cycle of happiness for you and others. (Page 74)

Chapter 6: Fearlessly Facing Change
1. Embracing Life's Curveballs: Why change is inevitable and how to navigate it with grace and resilience. (Page 81)

2. The Silver Lining: Finding the opportunities in change and using them to grow and evolve. (Page 83)

3. The Growth Mindset: Adopting a mindset that welcomes change and cultivates personal growth. (Page 86)

4. Bouncing Back: How to recover from setbacks and turn them into comebacks. (Page 89)

Chapter 7: Daring to Dream Big

1. The Power of Vision: How to set audacious goals and create a roadmap to achieve them. (Page 95)

2. Overcoming Self-Doubt: Strategies to silence your inner critic and unleash your full potential. (Page 98)

3. The Art of Hustle: Channeling your passion and drive into tangible results. (Page 100)

4. The Success Mindset: Developing a mindset that attracts success and happiness. (Page 102)

Chapter 8: Living Life, Doing Good, Being Happy

1. The Ultimate Balance: How to create a life that balances passion, purpose, and happiness. (Page 107)

2. The Power of Giving: Why doing good for others can bring immense happiness and fulfillment. (Page 110)

3. Crafting Your Legacy: How to make a lasting impact on the world and leave it better than you found it. (Page 112)

4. The Happiness Manifesto: A guide to living life to the fullest, doing good, and finding your path to happiness. (Page 115)

Chapter 9: Unleashing Your Inner Rebel

1. The Maverick Mindset: How to think outside the box and challenge conventional wisdom. (Page 121)

2. Breaking the Rules: Knowing when to defy societal norms and forge your own path. (Page 123)

3. Creativity Unleashed: Unlocking your unique talents and embracing your inner artist. (Page 126)

4. Innovate or Die: How to stay ahead of the curve and constantly reinvent yourself. (Page 128)

Chapter 10: The Power of Vulnerability

1. The Strength in Softness: Embracing vulnerability as a source of courage and connection. (Page 135)

2. Ditching the Armor: Letting go of emotional barriers and opening up to deeper connections. (Page 137)

3. The Authenticity Advantage: How being genuine and vulnerable can lead to greater success and happiness. (Page 140)

4. Healing Through Vulnerability: Using openness and self-expression as a path to healing and growth. (Page 141)

Chapter 11: Mastering Mindfulness

1. The Zen Zone: An introduction to mindfulness and its benefits for well-being and happiness. (Page 146)

2. Mindfulness in Motion: Practical techniques for incorporating mindfulness into everyday life. (Page 148)

3. The Power of Now: How to be fully present and engaged in each moment. (Page 150)

4. Mindful Relationships: Cultivating deeper connections and empathy through mindfulness. (Page 152)

Chapter 12: The Art of Letting Go

1. The Freedom of Forgiveness: Learning to forgive yourself and others for a happier, healthier life. (Page 157)

2. The Minimalist Mentality: Embracing simplicity and decluttering your life for more peace and focus. (Page 159)

3. Letting Go of Control: How to trust the process and surrender to the flow of life. (Page 162)

4. The Serenity of Acceptance: Finding peace and happiness by accepting what you cannot change. (Page 164)

Chapter 13: Building Bulletproof Confidence

1. Unshakable Self-Belief: Developing a rock-solid foundation of self-confidence. (Page 169)

2. The Confidence-Action Loop: How taking action can boost your confidence and create a positive feedback loop. (Page 171)

3. Owning Your Success: Celebrating your achievements and giving yourself the credit you deserve. (Page 173)

4. The Charisma Factor: Cultivating the magnetic presence that comes with authentic confidence. (Page 175)

Chapter 14: The Joy of Discomfort
1. The Comfort Zone Trap: Understanding the limitations of staying in your comfort zone. (Page 180)

2. The Growth-Pain Connection: How discomfort can lead to personal growth and transformation. (Page 183)

3. Becoming Comfortable with Discomfort: Embracing new challenges and pushing your boundaries. (Page 185)

4. The Reward of Resilience: Building mental toughness and resilience through overcoming adversity. (Page 187)

Chapter 15: The Life-Changing Power of Habits
1. Habit Hacking: How to build powerful habits that lead to success and happiness. (Page 193)

2. The Keystone Habits: Identifying the habits that have the greatest impact on your life. (Page 195)

3. The Habit Loop: Understanding the science behind habit formation and change. (Page 197)

4. Breaking Bad: Strategies for replacing negative habits with positive ones. (Page 199)

Chapter 16: The Pursuit of Passion
1. Igniting the Fire Within: Discovering your passions and finding your true calling. (Page 204)

2. The Passion-Drive Connection: How following your passions can fuel your motivation and success. (Page 206)

3. Integrating Passion into Your Life: Creating a lifestyle that supports and nurtures your passions. (Page 209)

4. The Ripple Effect of Passion: How pursuing your passions can inspire others and make a positive impact on the world. (Page 211)

Chapter 17: Nurturing Your Mental Health

1. The Mind-Body Connection: Understanding the link between mental health and overall well-being. (Page 216)

2. Mindful Self-Compassion: Cultivating a kind and caring relationship with yourself. (Page 218)

3. Stress-Busting Strategies: Techniques for managing stress and preventing burnout. (Page 220)

4. Seeking Support: Recognizing when to ask for help and building a strong support network. (Page 223)

Chapter 18: The Power of Positivity

1. The Optimism Advantage: How cultivating a positive mindset can enhance your life and happiness. (Page 228)

2. Rewiring Your Brain: Techniques for fostering positive thinking and overcoming negative thought patterns. (Page 231)

3. The Law of Attraction: Harnessing the power of positivity to manifest your desires. (Page 234)

4. Paying It Forward: Spreading positivity and kindness to create a happier, more connected world. (Page 236)

Chapter 19: The Art of Effective Communication

1. The Power of Active Listening: Developing the skills to truly hear and understand others. (Page 241)

2. The Gift of Empathy: Building deeper connections through compassionate communication. (Page 244)

3. Assertiveness Unleashed: Balancing confidence and respect in your communication style. (Page 246)

4. Conflict Resolution: Strategies for navigating disagreements and finding common ground. (Page 249)

Chapter 20: Crafting Your Life's Masterpiece

1. The Power of Intention: Setting a clear vision for the life you want to create. (Page 254)

2. The Mosaic of Experiences: Weaving together a rich tapestry of meaningful moments. (Page 257)

3. The Legacy Blueprint: Designing a life that leaves a lasting impact on the world. (Page 259)

4. The Final Chapter: Embracing the journey of life and finding joy in the pursuit of happiness, growth, and adventure. (Page 261)

Message from Mickey (Page 267)

KICKASS Exercise Cheat Sheet (Page 270)

Final Message from Mickey: (Page 278)

KICKASS Resources (Page 279)

Stay Connected (Page 283)

Chapter 1: Embracing Your Badass Self

Section 1: F*ck the Expectations: Why it's crucial to stop living life by other people's standards and start living for yourself.

Let's face it, life can be tough. From the moment we're born, we're bombarded with a set of expectations imposed on us by society, our families, and even ourselves. We're told that we should go to school, get good grades, get a job, settle down, have kids, and the list goes on. It's a never-ending cycle that can leave us feeling trapped and unfulfilled.

But what if I told you that it's time to break free from those expectations? That it's time to say "f*ck it" to living life by other people's standards and start living for yourself?

To truly embrace your badass self, you need to recognize that your life is your own. You don't have to follow a predetermined path, and you definitely don't need to live by anyone else's standards. As the legendary Steve Jobs once said, "Your time is limited, don't waste it living someone else's life."

But breaking free from expectations can be easier said than done. It's natural to feel like we need to live up to certain expectations, whether it's what our parents expect of us, societal norms, or self-imposed limitations. So, how can you break free from these chains and start living life on your own terms?

1. Identify the expectations that have been holding you back.

Take a step back and think about the expectations that have been weighing on you. Is it pressure from your family to pursue a certain career path? Are you afraid to pursue your passions because of societal norms? Are you limiting yourself because of self-doubt and fear of failure? Once you identify the expectations that have been holding you back, you can start to challenge them.

2. Ask yourself what YOU truly want.

This might be the most important step. What do you want out of life? What are your passions and what makes you happy? What kind of life do you envision for yourself? It's easy to get caught up in what others expect of us, but it's important to remember that your life is your own, and you deserve to live it the way you want.

3. Set your own goals and take the necessary steps to achieve them.

Once you know what you want, it's time to set your own goals and take action to achieve them. This might involve stepping out of your comfort zone, taking risks, and learning from your mistakes. It won't be easy, but it will be worth it.

4. Surround yourself with like minded people who support your journey and share your values.

Having a support network is essential when you're breaking free from expectations. Surround yourself with people who encourage you to pursue your dreams, who lift you up when you're feeling down, and who share your values. These are the people who will help you stay on track and remind you that you're capable of anything.

As you start living life on your own terms, you'll begin to discover the freedom and happiness that comes with embracing your badass self. Remember, as Oprah Winfrey once said, "You are responsible for your life. You can't keep blaming somebody else for your dysfunction." It's time to take ownership of your life, break free from expectations, and live like the badass you were meant to be.

Section 2: The Art of Being Unapologetically You: How to embrace your true self and not give a damn about societal norms.

Society has a way of trying to mold us into something we're not, but it's time to break free and be unapologetically YOU. Your quirks, your passions, your unique talents - they all make you who you are, and that's something to celebrate. But it can be challenging to embrace your true self fully, especially when societal norms and expectations are constantly weighing on us. Here are some tips on how to start being unapologetically you:

1. Practice self-awareness: The first step in embracing your true self is getting to know yourself better. Take time to reflect on your strengths, weaknesses, likes, and dislikes. Write them down, keep a journal, or meditate on them. The better you know yourself, the easier it is to embrace who you are and what makes you unique.

2. Be authentic: Don't be afraid to express your opinions, even if they're unpopular. Stand up for your beliefs and values, and don't compromise them just to fit in. It's okay to be different, and being true to yourself is more important than trying to please everyone else.

3. Embrace your imperfections: Nobody's perfect, and that's okay! Recognize that your flaws make you human and relatable. Instead of trying to hide them, own them, and embrace them. As the great Leonard Cohen said, "There is a crack in everything, that's how the light gets in."

4. Don't seek approval: It's human nature to want to be liked and accepted, but seeking approval from others can be a trap. You can't please everyone, so stop trying. Focus on pleasing yourself and living a life that aligns with your values.

5. Surround yourself with positive influences: Building a support network of people who lift you up and encourage you to believe in yourself is essential. Avoid people who bring you down, criticize you, or try to change you. Instead, seek out people who appreciate you for who you are and inspire you to be the best version of yourself.

6. Practice self-love: Self-love is crucial for embracing your true self. Treat yourself with kindness, respect, and compassion. Focus on your strengths, celebrate your accomplishments, and forgive yourself for your

mistakes. Practice gratitude and appreciation for everything that makes you unique.

Exercise: To help you on your journey to becoming unapologetically you, try this exercise:

Make a list of five things you love about yourself that others might consider "weird" or "unconventional." Embrace these aspects of yourself and recognize that they make you unique. Then, make a list of five things that you've always wanted to do or try but were too afraid to pursue. Start taking steps towards those goals and embrace the journey, even if it's challenging.

Remember, the more you embrace your true self, the happier and more fulfilled you'll be. Don't let societal norms and expectations hold you back from living the life you want. Be unapologetically you, and the world will celebrate you for it.

Section 3: Powering Through Impostor Syndrome: Why you're more than enough and how to own your greatness.

Impostor Syndrome is a sneaky little bastard that can make even the most accomplished person feel like a fraud. It's that voice in your head that tells you that you don't belong, that you're not smart enough, or that you're not worthy of your successes. But here's the thing - that voice is full of crap. You ARE enough, and it's time to kick Impostor Syndrome's ass and own your greatness.

First things first, it's important to recognize that Impostor Syndrome is a common experience, and you are not alone in feeling this way. In fact, research suggests that up to 70% of people experience Impostor Syndrome at some point in their lives.

But just because it's common doesn't mean you have to put up with it. Here are some kickass ways to tackle Impostor Syndrome head-on:

1. Acknowledge your accomplishments: It's easy to brush off your successes and focus on your mistakes or shortcomings. But to kick Impostor Syndrome's ass, you need to give yourself credit where credit is due. Make a list of all your accomplishments, big and small, and remind yourself of them regularly. Celebrate your wins and give yourself a pat on the back.

2. Flip the script: When you catch yourself thinking negative thoughts or beliefs about yourself, flip them around into positive affirmations. For example, if you're thinking, "I'm not good enough for this job," flip it to, "I am more than qualified for this job, and I have the skills and experience to excel." Repeat these affirmations to yourself daily, and watch your mindset shift.

3. Challenge your thoughts: Impostor Syndrome is often fueled by self-doubt and negative self-talk. When you catch yourself thinking unkind thoughts about yourself, challenge them. Ask yourself if these thoughts are based on facts or just your own insecurities. And if it's the latter, kick those thoughts to the curb and replace them with positive affirmations.

4. Surround yourself with positivity: Your environment can have a huge impact on your mindset. Surround yourself with people who lift you up and encourage you to believe in yourself. Seek out mentors or role models who have achieved what you aspire to achieve. And if necessary, distance yourself from people or situations that bring you down.

5. Embrace vulnerability: One of the biggest drivers of Impostor Syndrome is the fear of being exposed as a fraud. But here's the thing - everyone has flaws and makes mistakes. Embrace your vulnerabilities and own them. Being vulnerable is a sign of strength, not weakness.

Now, let's kick it up a notch with some exercises to help you kick Impostor Syndrome's ass:

1. Write a badass resume: Take some time to write a resume that truly showcases your accomplishments and skills. Don't hold back - this is your chance to brag about yourself. Once you've written it, read it over and over again until you start to believe just how kickass you are.

2. Keep a gratitude journal: Each day, write down three things you're grateful for. They can be big or small, but they should be things that make you feel good about yourself. This exercise will help you focus on the positive and build self-confidence.

3. Practice affirmations: Write down some positive affirmations that resonate with you and read them aloud each day. If you're not sure where to start, try "I am enough," "I deserve success," or "I am capable of achieving my goals."

Remember, Impostor Syndrome is a liar, and you are more than enough. Kick its ass and own your greatness. Don't let that sneaky little voice hold you back from achieving your goals and living your best life. You are capable, talented, and deserving of success. So, go out there and show Impostor Syndrome who's boss!

Here are a few more kickass tips to help you overcome Impostor Syndrome:

Set realistic expectations: It's easy to fall into the trap of setting impossibly high standards for yourself, which can feed into feelings of inadequacy. Instead, set realistic expectations for yourself and celebrate each step towards your goals. Remember, progress is more important than perfection.

Fake it 'til you make it: Confidence is a skill that can be developed, even if you don't feel confident yet. So, even if you don't feel like you're the expert in the room, act as if you are. Speak up, offer your opinions, and take risks. The more you practice confidence, the more natural it will become.

Take action: The longer you sit in your comfort zone, the louder Impostor Syndrome's voice becomes. So, take action towards your goals, even if it's just a small step. The more you do, the more evidence you have that you're capable of achieving great things.

Now, let's finish this section with one more kickass exercise to help you overcome Impostor Syndrome:

Create a "brag sheet": Make a list of all the compliments, positive feedback, and thank-you notes you've received throughout your life. They can be from coworkers, bosses, family members, friends, or anyone who's expressed gratitude or admiration towards you. Keep this list somewhere handy, and refer to it often to remind yourself of your strengths and achievements.

Remember, Impostor Syndrome is just a feeling, not a fact. You are capable, you are worthy, and you are enough. So, kick its ass and own your greatness.

Section 4: The Confidence Catalyst: How building self-confidence can transform your life and help you conquer your fears.

Confidence is the key to unlocking your full potential and living your best life. When you believe in yourself, you're more likely to take risks, pursue your dreams, and overcome challenges. But building confidence isn't always easy, especially if you've struggled with self-doubt or insecurities in the past.

The good news is that confidence is a skill that can be learned and strengthened over time. Here are some kickass strategies for building unstoppable confidence:

1. Take Action: One of the best ways to build confidence is to take action towards your goals. Set realistic, achievable goals and break them down into smaller steps. Celebrate each milestone you reach, no matter how small it may seem. By taking action towards your goals, you'll build momentum and develop a sense of accomplishment that will boost your confidence.

2. Embrace Failure: Failure is a natural part of the learning process and a stepping stone to success. Instead of fearing failure, embrace it and learn from it. Recognize that every failure is an opportunity to grow, learn, and improve. Remember, even the most successful people have failed multiple times before achieving their goals.

3. Focus on Your Strengths: It's easy to get caught up in our weaknesses or areas for improvement, but to build unstoppable confidence, it's important to focus on our strengths. Take time to identify your unique skills, talents, and experiences. When you focus on what you're good at, you'll feel more confident and capable of achieving your goals.

4. Practice Self-Compassion: Treat yourself with kindness and understanding, just like you would treat a close friend. Be gentle with yourself and avoid negative self-talk or self-criticism. When you practice self-compassion, you'll develop a more positive outlook and a stronger sense of self-worth.

5. Visualize Success: Visualization is a powerful tool for building confidence and achieving your goals. Spend time each day visualizing yourself succeeding in your goals and overcoming obstacles. Imagine the feeling of accomplishment and satisfaction you'll experience once you achieve your goals. By visualizing success, you'll program your mind to focus on positive outcomes and develop an unwavering belief in your abilities.

To help you build unstoppable confidence, try these kickass exercises:

- Write a Confidence List: Make a list of all the things that make you feel confident, whether it's a skill, an accomplishment, or a personal quality. Refer to this list whenever you need a confidence boost.

- Dress for Success: Choose an outfit that makes you feel confident and wear it whenever you need to feel empowered or assertive.

- Keep a Success Journal: Write down your successes and accomplishments, no matter how small they may seem. Reflect on them regularly to remind yourself of your capabilities and build momentum towards your goals.

- Stand in Your Power Pose: Stand tall with your feet shoulder-width apart, place your hands on your hips, and lift your chin up. Hold this pose for two minutes, taking deep breaths and feeling the confidence surge through your body.

- The Mirror Challenge: Look yourself in the eye and tell yourself five things you love about yourself. It can be anything from your sense of humor, your intelligence, or your determination. Repeat this exercise every day for a week and notice how it makes you feel.
- The Gratitude Jar: Write down something that you're grateful for every day on a slip of paper and put it in a jar. Whenever you need a confidence boost, take out a slip of paper and read it to remind yourself of all the good things in your life.
- The Power Stance: Stand tall with your feet shoulder-width apart and place your hands on your hips. Take deep breaths and hold this pose for two minutes. Imagine yourself as a confident, badass warrior ready to take on any challenge.

Remember, building self-confidence is a journey, not a destination. It takes time, effort, and practice, but the rewards are worth it. So, go out there, unleash your inner confidence beast, and kick ass in every aspect of your life.

Kickass Bonus Content: The Fearless Formula

Want to take your badassery to the next level? Try out this Fearless Formula to tackle your fears and take on the world:

1. Identify your fears: Make a list of everything that's holding you back or causing you anxiety.

2. Analyze your fears: Ask yourself, "What's the worst that could happen?" Often, you'll realize that the consequences are not as dire as you imagined.

3. Face your fears head-on: Confront each fear one by one, either by taking a small step to overcome it or by fully diving in.

4. Reflect on the experience: After facing your fear, take some time to reflect on what you've learned and how it's helped you grow.

5. Rinse and repeat: Continue to face your fears and challenge yourself regularly, knowing that you're becoming a more fearless, badass version of yourself with each step.

Chapter 1 Summary: Embracing Your Badass Self

In this chapter, we explored the importance of breaking free from societal expectations, embracing your true self, overcoming Impostor Syndrome, and building self-confidence. By following the guidance and exercises provided, you'll be well on your way to becoming a fearless, unstoppable force.

Five KICKASS Questions to Reflect on:

1. What societal expectations have been holding you back from embracing your badass self?

2. What are some unique qualities or traits that make you unapologetically you, and how can you celebrate them more often?

3. How has Impostor Syndrome affected your life, and what steps can you take to overcome it?

4. In what areas of your life do you need to build more confidence, and what actions can you take to strengthen that confidence muscle?

5. Which of your fears are you ready to face head-on, and how will you use the Fearless Formula to tackle them?

Chapter 2: Life-Changing Magic of Saying "No"

Section 1: The 'No' Mindset: How saying no can open up more opportunities for growth and success.

Welcome to the world of badassery, where setting boundaries is the magical potion that will change your life and send your happiness soaring to new heights. We're about to dive into the KICKASS realm of limits, and trust me, you're going to love it.

When you set boundaries, you're essentially drawing a line in the sand that says, "This is what I need to feel happy, healthy, and fulfilled. Anything beyond this line is a no-go zone." It's the ultimate form of self-care, and it's something that every badass individual should embrace.

Here's why setting boundaries is so crucial:

1. It protects your energy: You know those people who just seem to suck the life out of you? By setting boundaries, you can keep those energy vampires at bay and ensure that you're only investing your time and energy in relationships that uplift and support you.

2. It boosts your self-esteem: When you set boundaries, you're sending a powerful message to yourself and others that your needs, feelings, and well-being are important. This, in turn, strengthens your self-esteem and makes you feel like the KICKASS human you are.

3. It fosters healthier relationships: Boundaries aren't just good for you – they're also essential for creating

healthy, respectful relationships with others. When both parties have a clear understanding of each other's limits, it paves the way for more open communication and deeper connections.

Now that you know why boundaries are so important, let's talk about how you can start setting them in your own life. Here are some KICKASS strategies to help you set limits like a pro:

1. Get clear on your values: The first step to setting boundaries is to understand what you truly value in life. Make a list of your core values, and use this as a guide when deciding what you're willing to accept and what's a deal-breaker.

2. Practice assertive communication: Being able to express your boundaries clearly and confidently is crucial. This means speaking up when something doesn't feel right, and saying "no" when necessary. Remember, you're a badass – don't be afraid to stand your ground.

3. Be prepared for pushback: Not everyone will be thrilled with your newfound boundaries, and that's okay. Stay firm, and remind yourself that you're setting limits for your own well-being.

4. Reevaluate and adjust: Setting boundaries is an ongoing process. As you grow and change, so will your limits. Regularly check in with yourself to ensure that your boundaries are still serving you well.

To wrap things up, let me leave you with a quote from the legendary Brené Brown: "Daring to set boundaries is about having the courage to love ourselves, even when we risk disappointing others." Embrace the magic of boundaries, and watch your life transform in KICKASS ways you never thought possible.

Section 2: Prioritize Like a Boss: Strategies for effectively managing your time and energy by saying no to what doesn't serve you.

I get it. Saying "no" can feel like a daunting task, especially when you don't want to hurt someone's feelings or burn bridges. But worry not, my friend! I'm here to show you how to say "no" with tact, diplomacy, and compassion – like a KICKASS diplomat of your own life.

1. Be honest, but not brutal: Honesty is always the best policy, but you don't have to be brutally honest. For instance, if you're invited to an event you're not interested in, don't say, "That sounds boring as hell." Instead, try something like, "I appreciate the invite, but it's not really my thing. I hope you have a great time, though!" See? You've said "no" without being a jerk.

2. Show empathy: Put yourself in the other person's shoes and let them know you understand their feelings. Saying something like, "I know you were really counting on me, but I can't commit to this right now," shows that you recognize the impact of your "no" and that you care about their feelings.

3. Offer an alternative (if possible): If you can't say "yes" to a specific request, see if you can find a way to help in another capacity. For example, if a friend asks you to help them move but you're swamped with work, suggest helping them pack or lending them your truck. It's a KICKASS way to show that you care while still saying "no" to the initial request.

4. Use the "sandwich" technique: Who doesn't love a good sandwich? The sandwich technique involves layering a "no" between two positive statements. Start by acknowledging the request or offering a compliment, then deliver your "no," and finish with another positive statement. For example: "I'm flattered that you thought of me for this project, but I'm not able to take it on right now. I'm sure you'll find someone great to help you out, though!"

5. Keep it simple: You don't need to provide an elaborate explanation for every "no." Sometimes, a simple, "I can't commit to that right now" or "I have other priorities at the moment" is enough. You're not obligated to justify your decisions to everyone – remember, you're a KICKASS individual with your own goals and boundaries.

6. Practice, practice, practice: Like any skill, graceful rejection takes practice. The more you flex your "no" muscle, the easier it will become. Start by saying "no" to smaller, less consequential requests and work your way

up. You'll soon be a master of the art of saying "no" with grace and compassion.

By mastering the art of graceful rejection, you'll maintain your integrity and relationships while still protecting your time, energy, and priorities. That's what I call KICKASS diplomacy! So go forth, and confidently say "no" with tact, diplomacy, and compassion.

Section 3: The No-F*cks-Given Guide to Setting Boundaries: Protecting your peace of mind and establishing healthy personal boundaries.

Listen up, my friend! Overcoming the guilt trip is an essential part of embracing the KICKASS 'No' Mindset. You're going to face people who try to manipulate you into saying "yes" when you really want to say "no." But you're not here to please everyone. You're here to live your best damn life, and you can't do that if you're constantly bending to the whims of others.

First, let's talk about recognizing manipulation. Manipulators come in many forms — they can be family, friends, coworkers, or even strangers. They might make you feel guilty, selfish, or unkind for saying "no." But here's the truth: you're not responsible for their feelings or reactions. You're responsible for your own life, and you have every right to say "no" when it's in your best interest.

So how can you overcome the guilt trip and stand your ground like a KICKASS hero? Here are some strategies:

1. Be assertive: Communicate your boundaries clearly and confidently. Remember, you have the right to say "no," and you don't need to justify your decision. Keep your response short and sweet — something like, "I appreciate the offer, but I'm not able to commit to that right now."

2. Don't apologize for saying "no": Apologizing implies that you've done something wrong, which feeds into the manipulator's guilt trip. Stand tall and own your decision.

3. Practice self-compassion: It's normal to feel guilty when you say "no," especially if you're used to being a people-pleaser. Recognize that these feelings are a natural part of the process, and remind yourself that it's okay to prioritize your own well-being.

4. Surround yourself with supportive people: Build a network of friends, family, and mentors who respect your boundaries and encourage your growth. These are the people who will cheer you on as you take control of your life.

Here's a KICKASS exercise to help you overcome the guilt trip: The next time someone tries to manipulate you into saying "yes," take a deep breath and visualize yourself as a superhero with a shield that deflects their guilt-inducing words. Remind yourself of your goals and values, and respond assertively without apologizing or over-explaining.

As the legendary poet Maya Angelou said, "When someone shows you who they are, believe them the first time." If someone consistently tries to manipulate you, it's time to reevaluate that relationship and consider whether it's worth keeping in your life.

By overcoming the guilt trip and standing your ground, you're taking control of your life and living it on your own KICKASS terms. Don't let anyone else hold you back – you've got this!

Section 4: The Rewards of Saying No: How embracing the power of rejection can unlock a world of freedom, self-respect, and personal growth.

Alright, you've reached the grand finale – the crowning glory of the KICKASS journey towards embracing the power of "no." It's time to reap the rewards of all the "no's" you've been dishing out, and let me tell you, these rewards are sweeter than a candy store on Halloween.

First up, let's talk about freedom. Saying "no" is like breaking free from a prison of obligations and expectations. As you start rejecting the things that don't serve you, you'll notice a profound sense of liberation. Suddenly, you're in control of your life, and you get to choose how you spend your time and energy. That, my friend, is the taste of pure, unadulterated freedom.

Next, we have self-respect. By setting boundaries and sticking to your guns, you're sending a clear message to yourself and others: "I know my worth, and I won't settle for anything less."

It's like standing atop a mountain, declaring your awesomeness to the world. Self-respect is the KICKASS foundation of a strong and unshakable sense of self.

Finally, we arrive at personal growth. When you say "no" to the things that hold you back, you make room for experiences and opportunities that align with your goals and values. Embracing the power of rejection is like planting seeds in the fertile soil of your life, and with time and nurturing, these seeds will grow into a lush garden of personal development.

So, how do you start reaping these KICKASS rewards? It's simple. keep practicing the art of saying "no." Stay true to your priorities, maintain healthy boundaries, and never forget the value of your time and energy. As you continue to embrace the power of rejection, you'll unlock a world of freedom, self-respect, and personal growth that's waiting just for you.

To help you along the way, try this final exercise: Write a list of three rewards you hope to gain from saying "no" more often. Keep this list somewhere visible, like on your bathroom mirror or your phone's wallpaper, as a constant reminder of the KICKASS life you're working towards.

Remember, the power of "no" is within you. Embrace it, and watch as your life transforms into the KICKASS adventure you've always dreamed of.

Kickass Bonus Content: The Badass No-Brainer Decision Matrix

Struggling to decide when to say yes and when to say no? Try using the Badass No-Brainer Decision Matrix to simplify the process:

1. List your top priorities and values.

2. For each request or opportunity, ask yourself:

    - Does it align with my priorities or values?

    - Will it bring me closer to my goals or personal growth?

    - Do I have the time, energy, and resources to commit to it?

3. If the answer to all three questions is "yes," go for it! If not, confidently say no and move on.

This simple decision-making tool will help you quickly and confidently determine when to say yes and when to say no, like a true badass.

Chapter 2 Summary: The Power of Saying No

In this chapter, we delved into the importance of setting boundaries, the art of graceful rejection, overcoming guilt trips, and the rewards of saying no. With these insights and exercises, you're now equipped to stand your ground, protect your priorities, and live life on your terms.

Five KICKASS Questions to Reflect on:

1. In what areas of your life do you struggle to set boundaries, and how can you improve in those areas?

2. How can you practice the art of graceful rejection to say no without burning bridges?

3. What strategies can you use to recognize and overcome guilt trips when setting boundaries?

4. Which benefits of saying no resonate most with you, and how can you harness these rewards in your life?

5. How can the Badass No-Brainer Decision Matrix help you make better choices about when to say yes and when to say no?

Chapter 3: Building Kickass Connections

Section 1: The Science of Genuine Connection: Understanding the power of authentic relationships and their impact on happiness.

Let me start by saying, KICKASS connections are the backbone of a fulfilling life! Genuine connections are so powerful that they have the ability to transform your life and skyrocket your happiness levels. It's time to dive into the science behind these authentic relationships to help you understand why they are so essential to your journey. Grab a drink, get cozy, and let's get into it!

To understand the science of genuine connection, we must first grasp the concept of authenticity. Authenticity is about being true to yourself, your values, and your beliefs, without wearing a mask or conforming to others' expectations. When you can be your true self, you can form authentic connections with others who share similar values and beliefs, creating a strong foundation for lasting relationships.

Several scientific studies have shown the benefits of genuine connections, both on our mental health and overall well-being. Here are some KICKASS findings:

1. Strong social connections lead to a 50% increased chance of longevity. It's not rocket science, folks! When you're surrounded by people who care for you and vice versa, you're more likely to live a longer, happier life. A study by the American Psychological Association

concluded that having solid social connections could even have a more significant impact on your lifespan than factors like obesity and smoking.

2. Authentic relationships improve mental health. Feeling supported and understood by others helps in reducing anxiety, depression, and stress. According to a study published in the Journal of Social and Personal Relationships, people with strong social connections have better mental health than those with weaker or superficial connections.

3. Genuine connections boost self-esteem. Knowing that you have a tribe of people who love and accept you for who you are can do wonders for your self-esteem. It helps you believe in yourself and your abilities, making you more resilient in the face of life's challenges.

Now that we've seen the KICKASS impact of genuine connections on our well-being, let's talk about how to build and foster these relationships.

First, be vulnerable. Opening up about your thoughts, feelings, and experiences allows others to connect with you on a deeper level. As Brené Brown, the queen of vulnerability, said, "Vulnerability is the birthplace of connection and the path to the feeling of worthiness." So, take off that mask and share your true self with the world.

Second, practice empathy. When you can truly understand and share the feelings of another person, you create a strong emotional bond. Empathy allows you to support others in their journey and be there for them when they need you most.

Finally, be present. In the age of smartphones and constant distractions, being fully present when interacting with others is a rare gift. Actively listening and engaging in conversations without getting lost in your thoughts or checking your phone demonstrates genuine interest and creates stronger connections.

Here's a KICKASS exercise for you: Write down three people in your life with whom you'd like to build a deeper connection. Reach out to them this week and invite them for a coffee or a walk. Focus on being vulnerable, empathetic, and present during your time together. You'll be amazed at how your relationships transform!

That's it for Section 1, folks! Remember, authentic relationships are the foundation of a KICKASS life. Embrace your true self, and don't be afraid to create and nurture genuine connections. Up next is Section 2: Networking for the Soul, where we'll dive into how to make meaningful connections beyond superficial encounters. Let's keep this KICKASS momentum going!

Section 2: Networking for the Soul: How to create meaningful connections beyond superficial encounters.

Welcome back, my KICKASS friend! In this section, we're going to explore Networking for the Soul – a concept that's all about creating deep, meaningful connections instead of just collecting business cards or friend requests. Let's dive in and learn how to connect with others on a soul level!

1. Start with a KICKASS mindset: Networking for the Soul begins with a mindset shift. Instead of viewing networking as a chore or a way to benefit yourself, approach it as an opportunity to build genuine relationships and add value to others' lives. When you come from a place of authenticity, curiosity, and generosity, you'll naturally attract like-minded people who resonate with your energy.

2. Quality over quantity: Forget about trying to meet as many people as possible at an event or on social media. Focus on having deeper conversations and creating stronger connections with a few individuals. In the wise words of Maya Angelou, "People will forget what you said, people will forget what you did, but people will never forget how you made them feel." Make each interaction count by being present, attentive, and genuinely interested in others.

3. Be the first to open up: When you share your stories, thoughts, and emotions, you create a space for others to do the same. This reciprocal vulnerability can lead to powerful connections that go beyond superficial chit-chat. As you open up, remember that it's essential to strike a balance between sharing and listening. Be mindful not to monopolize the conversation or overshare, as it may overwhelm the other person.

4. Find common ground: To create a lasting connection, look for shared interests, values, or experiences. This will give you a starting point for deeper conversations and help you establish a bond with the other person. Don't be afraid to ask open-ended questions and genuinely listen to their answers.

5. Follow up with intention: After you've met someone and had a meaningful conversation, don't let that connection fade away. Reach out to them and express your appreciation for the encounter. You can also invite them to join you in an activity related to your shared interests or simply check in on them from time to time. This helps nurture the connection and shows that you genuinely care about the relationship.

Here's a KICKASS exercise to help you practice Networking for the Soul: The next time you attend an event or engage with people on social media, focus on having a few deeper conversations rather than trying to meet everyone. Be authentic, share your stories, and actively listen to what the other person has to say. Afterward, follow up with those individuals and continue building the connection.

And that's a wrap for Section 2! Networking for the Soul is all about creating genuine, meaningful connections that nourish your spirit and enrich your life. Keep these principles in mind, and you'll be well on your way to building a KICKASS network of soulful connections. Stay tuned for Section 3: Nurturing Your Tribe, where we'll dive into strategies for maintaining and strengthening your relationships with your inner circle. Let's keep this KICKASS journey going!

Section 3: Nurturing Your Tribe: Strategies for maintaining and strengthening your relationships with your inner circle.

Congratulations! You've made it this far, which means you're serious about making KICKASS connections in your life. In this section, we're going to explore how to nurture and strengthen your relationships with your tribe — the people who've got your back, no matter what. Let's dive in!

1. Communicate openly and honestly: Healthy communication is the lifeblood of any KICKASS relationship. Make a conscious effort to share your thoughts and feelings with your tribe regularly. Encourage them to do the same. Remember that communication is a two-way street — listen actively and engage with empathy.

2. Show appreciation: Never underestimate the power of gratitude. Express your appreciation for your tribe by acknowledging their efforts, support, and love. A simple "thank you" or a heartfelt compliment can go a long way in nurturing your relationships.

3. Create shared experiences: Shared experiences are the glue that holds your tribe together. Organize get-togethers, outings, or adventures with your inner circle. These memories will strengthen your bond and remind you of the good times when life gets tough.

4. Support personal growth: A KICKASS tribe is all about lifting each other up. Encourage your friends to pursue their passions, dreams, and goals. Offer your support, resources, and connections to help them grow, and celebrate their successes together.

5. Be reliable and dependable: Actions speak louder than words, my friends! Show your tribe that they can count on you by being there for them in times of need. Keep your promises, and always be willing to lend a helping hand.

6. Resolve conflicts with respect: Disagreements are bound to happen in any relationship. When they arise, tackle them head-on with open communication and respect. Remember that maintaining the relationship is more important than being right.

Here's another KICKASS exercise for you: Organize a monthly "Tribe Night" with your inner circle. This could be anything from a potluck dinner to a game night or a volunteer activity. The goal is to create shared experiences and nurture your relationships.

In conclusion, your tribe is your support system, your cheerleaders, and your partners in crime. By nurturing these relationships, you're not only building a network of people who genuinely care about you, but you're also investing in your own happiness and well-being. Keep these strategies in mind as you continue to grow and evolve with your tribe.

Stay tuned for the final section of this chapter, Section 4: Letting Go, where we'll discuss how to identify toxic or unfulfilling relationships and when it's time to cut ties and move on. Keep up the KICKASS work!

Section 4: Letting Go: Knowing when it's time to cut ties and move on from toxic or unfulfilling relationships.

Listen up, my KICKASS friends! While building and nurturing genuine connections is a huge part of a fulfilling life, it's equally important to recognize when it's time to let go of relationships that no longer serve you. Cutting ties with toxic or unfulfilling relationships can be a difficult process, but it's essential for your growth and happiness.

Here's how you can identify when it's time to move on from a relationship:

1. The relationship is draining your energy. If you feel exhausted, emotionally drained, or constantly stressed due to a specific relationship, it's a strong indication that it's time to reevaluate its place in your life. Your well-being should always come first, and relationships that suck the life out of you are simply not worth it.

2. Your values and goals have changed. People change, and sometimes our values and goals no longer align with those of our friends or partners. If you find yourself moving in a different direction than the other person, it might be time to part ways and continue on your own unique path.

3. You're constantly giving, but not receiving. A KICKASS relationship is built on mutual support and reciprocity. If you're always the one providing support, encouragement, or resources, but not receiving any in return, it might be time to reevaluate the relationship and consider moving on.

4. The relationship is filled with negativity. If your interactions with someone are primarily filled with negativity, criticism, or toxicity, it's a clear sign that the relationship is doing more harm than good. Surround yourself with positivity and let go of those who bring you down.

Now that you know when it's time to let go, let's talk about how to gracefully move on from toxic or unfulfilling relationships:

1. Be honest with yourself and the other person. Be brave and have an open conversation about your feelings and concerns. It's essential to express your thoughts and emotions in a respectful and assertive manner, without blaming or attacking the other person.

2. Set boundaries. If you've decided to end the relationship, make sure to establish clear boundaries to protect yourself and prevent future conflicts. This might include limiting communication or avoiding certain situations where you might encounter the person.

3. Focus on your personal growth. Take this opportunity to invest in yourself and your personal development.

Engage in activities that make you happy, set new goals, and surround yourself with supportive and positive people.

4. Practice self-compassion. Letting go of a relationship can be a painful process. Be kind to yourself and recognize that it's okay to grieve and feel a sense of loss. Allow yourself time to heal and process your emotions.

Here's a KICKASS exercise for you: Write down three relationships in your life that are draining your energy or no longer align with your values and goals. Reflect on the reasons why it might be time to move on, and create an action plan to gracefully end these relationships.

Remember, my KICKASS friends, letting go of toxic or unfulfilling relationships is an essential step in creating a fulfilling life. Embrace the process, focus on your personal growth, and never forget that you deserve nothing but the best. Now go out there and conquer the world with your KICKASS connections!

Kickass Bonus Content: The Relationship-Building Power Hour

Supercharge your connection-building efforts with this powerful Relationship-Building Power Hour. Dedicate just one hour per week to reach out, reconnect, and strengthen your relationships. Here's how:

1. Make a list of people you want to reconnect with or get to know better.

2. Schedule a weekly Power Hour to focus solely on relationship building.
3. During the Power Hour, send messages, make calls, or set up coffee dates with people on your list.

The Relationship-Building Power Hour will help you create and maintain meaningful connections, expand your network, and strengthen your tribe.

One other kickass thing you can do is to foster genuine connections, try this "Authenticity Audit" exercise:

- Make a list of your top five relationships (family, friends, romantic partners, etc.).
- For each person, rate the authenticity of your connection on a scale of 1 (superficial) to 10 (deeply genuine).
- Reflect on ways to deepen the connections that fall short of a 10 and create an action plan to improve those relationships.

Remember, genuine connections require ongoing effort and vulnerability. Embrace the science of connection and watch your happiness soar.

Chapter 3 Summary: Building Kickass Connections

In this chapter, we explored the science of genuine connection, networking for the soul, nurturing your tribe, and knowing when to let go of toxic or unfulfilling relationships. With these insights, exercises, and strategies, you're now equipped to create and maintain meaningful connections that enrich your life and contribute to your happiness.

Five KICKASS Questions to Reflect on:

1. How can you apply the principles of the science of genuine connection to deepen your relationships?

2. What strategies can you use to network for the soul and create meaningful connections beyond superficial encounters?

3. How will you prioritize nurturing your tribe and maintaining your most important relationships?

4. What signs can you look for to know when it's time to let go of a toxic or unfulfilling relationship?

5. How can you incorporate the Relationship-Building Power Hour into your routine to enhance your connection-building efforts?

Chapter 4: Embracing the Thrill of the Unknown

Section 1: The Adventure Mindset: How to approach life with a sense of curiosity and excitement, making every day an adventure.

Buckle up, grab your favorite pair of sneakers, and get ready for a KICKASS journey into the Adventure Mindset! Let's face it, life can become dull and monotonous if you don't infuse it with a little bit of excitement. So, how can you turn your daily routine into an exhilarating rollercoaster ride? The answer is simple: embrace the Adventure Mindset.

The Adventure Mindset is all about breaking free from the shackles of your everyday life and injecting a sense of curiosity, wonder, and excitement into every moment. Here are some KICKASS tips and tricks to help you unleash your inner adventurer and make every day a thrilling, awe-inspiring experience.

1. Say YES to New Experiences: Remember that iconic scene from the movie "Yes Man" where Jim Carrey's character decides to say yes to everything? Well, that's the kind of attitude you need to adopt if you want to dive headfirst into the Adventure Mindset. Open yourself up to new experiences, be it a spontaneous weekend getaway or trying out that weird-looking dish at the local food truck. Embrace the unfamiliar and watch your life transform into a KICKASS adventure.

2. Break Free from Routine: Routines can be comforting, but they can also lead to boredom and stagnation. Break free from the chains of monotony by mixing things up from time to time. Instead of hitting the gym after work, try going for a hike in the nearby forest or joining a dance class. Change the way you commute to work or explore a new part of town during your lunch break. You'll be amazed at how these small changes can make your life feel like an endless adventure.

3. Ask the Right Questions: Curiosity may have killed the cat, but it also fuels the Adventure Mindset. Start asking questions and sparking conversations with the people around you. Who knows, you might learn something new or make a lifelong friend in the process. Remember, every person you meet is a potential gateway to a whole new world of experiences and adventures.

4. Embrace Challenges: Challenges are the spice of life, and they're essential for keeping your mind sharp and your spirit strong. When you face a challenge head-on, you're not only proving your resilience but also opening the door to new opportunities and experiences. So, don't back down from a challenge – embrace it and use it as a springboard to propel yourself into a more KICKASS life.

5. Exercise Your Imagination: The world is your playground, and your imagination is the key to unlocking its hidden treasures. Get your creative juices flowing by

daydreaming, doodling, or coming up with wild stories. As Albert Einstein once said, "Imagination is everything. It is the preview of life's coming attractions." So, unleash your inner child and let your imagination run wild – you never know where it might take you.

6. Be Present: To truly embrace the Adventure Mindset, you must learn to live in the moment. Put down your phone, disconnect from the virtual world, and immerse yourself in the present. Life's greatest adventures often happen when you least expect them, so keep your eyes open, your senses sharp, and your heart ready to embrace whatever comes your way.

7. Surround Yourself with Adventurous People: You know the saying, "You are the average of the five people you spend the most time with"? Well, it's time to take a good look at your social circle and evaluate whether they're fueling your adventurous spirit or holding you back. Surround yourself with like-minded individuals who share your thirst for exploration and excitement. They will inspire you, support you, and push you to new heights in your KICKASS adventure-filled life.

8. Keep Learning and Growing: Adventure is not just about physical experiences; it's also about personal growth and self-discovery. Stay curious and never stop learning – pick up a new hobby, read books on a wide range of topics, or attend workshops to expand your skillset. By

continuously learning and growing, you'll keep your mind sharp and your sense of adventure alive.

9. Document Your Journey: A life filled with adventure is one worth remembering. So, whether you prefer journaling, photography, or vlogging, find a way to document your experiences and the lessons you've learned along the way. Not only will this serve as a reminder of how far you've come, but it will also inspire you to keep pushing forward and seeking new adventures.

10. Cultivate Gratitude: It's easy to get caught up in the thrill of new experiences, but don't forget to appreciate the beauty and wonder of the world around you. Practice gratitude by taking the time to reflect on your adventures and the memories you've created. This will help you stay grounded and remind you of just how KICKASS your life really is.

Adopting the Adventure Mindset is about breaking free from the confines of your comfort zone and daring to live a life filled with curiosity, excitement, and, of course, adventure. The world is a vast, beautiful, and endlessly fascinating place – so strap on your metaphorical explorer's hat and dive into the unknown. And And remember, as the great Helen Keller once said, "Life is either a daring adventure or nothing at all." So, don't settle for a mundane existence; embrace the Adventure Mindset and make every single day a KICKASS escapade worth remembering.

So, don't wait another moment – take that leap of faith, embrace the unknown, and start living your most KICKASS life today. The world is waiting for you, my friend. It's time to answer its call and embark on the adventure of a lifetime.

Section 2: Jumping Off the Comfort Cliff: The benefits of taking risks and stepping out of your comfort zone.

Alright, folks, it's time to talk about something that's absolutely crucial to living a KICKASS, adventure-filled life: jumping off the Comfort Cliff. You might be wondering what the heck I'm talking about, so let me break it down for you.

The Comfort Cliff is that metaphorical edge where your cozy, predictable life ends and the wild, untamed world of risk-taking begins. It's that moment when you decide to step out of your comfort zone and plunge into the exhilarating unknown. Sounds scary, right? But trust me, the benefits of jumping off the Comfort Cliff far outweigh the fear, and here's why:

1. Personal Growth: Taking risks and stepping out of your comfort zone is a surefire way to grow as a person. You'll be pushed to your limits, forced to confront your fears, and ultimately, you'll come out stronger and more resilient on the other side. As the legendary Robin Sharma once said, "Change is hard at first, messy in the middle, and gorgeous at the end."

2. Boosts Confidence: When you take a risk and succeed, your confidence soars to new heights. And even if you fail, you'll still gain valuable experience and the

knowledge that you had the courage to take a leap of faith. Remember, confidence isn't about always winning; it's about knowing you can handle whatever life throws your way.

3. Enhances Creativity: Stepping out of your comfort zone can open your mind to new ideas and perspectives, fostering creativity and innovation. By exposing yourself to unfamiliar situations, you'll be inspired to think outside the box and find unique solutions to problems.

4. Builds Resilience: The more you push yourself to take risks, the better equipped you'll be to bounce back from setbacks and adversity. Every time you jump off the Comfort Cliff, you're building your resilience muscle, making it easier to face challenges head-on in the future.

5. Expands Your Horizons: When you take risks and step out of your comfort zone, you'll inevitably encounter new experiences, people, and opportunities that you might never have discovered otherwise. This can lead to a richer, more fulfilling life filled with KICKASS adventures and unforgettable memories.

6. Increases Happiness: Stepping out of your comfort zone can be a major mood booster. When you take risks, your brain releases feel-good chemicals like dopamine and endorphins, giving you a natural high and a sense of accomplishment.

So, how can you start jumping off the Comfort Cliff and reaping these KICKASS benefits? Here are a few tips to get you started:

1. Start Small: You don't need to go skydiving or quit your job to step out of your comfort zone. Begin with small risks, like striking up a conversation with a stranger or trying a new workout routine. These baby steps will help you build the courage and confidence needed to tackle bigger challenges.

2. Embrace Discomfort: Make a conscious effort to seek out situations that make you feel uncomfortable or scared. The more you expose yourself to discomfort, the more comfortable you'll become with the unknown.

3. Set SMART Goals: When setting goals, make sure they're Specific, Measurable, Achievable, Relevant, and Time-bound (SMART). This will help you focus on the risks that are most likely to propel you towards your dreams and aspirations.

4. Find a Support System: Surround yourself with people who share your adventurous spirit and encourage you to take risks. They'll be there to cheer you on, offer guidance, and pick you up when you stumble.

Remember, the greatest rewards in life often lie just beyond the boundaries of your comfort zone. So, take a deep breath, muster up the courage, and jump off the Comfort Cliff. Embrace the unknown, face your fears, and push yourself to new heights. Before you know it, you'll be living a life filled with

KICKASS adventures, personal growth, and boundless happiness. Don't let fear hold you back – take the leap and start reaping the incredible benefits of stepping out of your comfort zone today. You've got this!

Section 3: The Art of Failing Forward: Learning from your failures and using them as stepping stones to success.

Get ready to embrace the KICKASS concept of Failing Forward. Failure is an inevitable part of life, but it's how you react to it that truly defines you. In this section, we're going to explore the Art of Failing Forward and how you can turn setbacks into stepping stones on your path to success.

1. Redefine Failure: First things first, let's change the way we think about failure. Failure is not the end; it's merely a detour on the road to success. Instead of seeing failure as a roadblock, view it as a valuable learning opportunity. With the right mindset, every failure becomes a chance to grow, improve, and come back stronger than ever.

2. Embrace the Lessons: Every failure carries a lesson, and it's up to you to decipher what that lesson is. Analyze your mistakes and pinpoint where things went wrong. Then, use that knowledge to refine your approach and prevent similar mistakes in the future. Remember, the most KICKASS individuals are those who learn from their failures and come back stronger than ever.

3. Keep Your Eyes on the Prize: When you encounter failure, it's essential to stay focused on your ultimate goal. Don't let setbacks derail your progress or dampen your enthusiasm. Keep your eyes firmly fixed on the prize and use your failures as motivation to push harder and reach even greater heights.

4. Develop Resilience: Failing Forward requires a healthy dose of resilience. The ability to bounce back from setbacks and persevere despite adversity is a crucial skill for anyone looking to lead a KICKASS life. Cultivate resilience by adopting a growth mindset, practicing self-compassion, and maintaining a strong support system of friends and family.

5. Don't Fear Failure: Fear of failure can be a significant obstacle in your pursuit of success. To truly master the Art of Failing Forward, you must learn to face failure head-on without fear. Embrace the uncertainty and remember that the greatest successes often come after a series of failures. As the legendary Michael Jordan said, "I've failed over and over and over again in my life. And that is why I succeed."

6. Celebrate Your Failures: It might sound counterintuitive, but celebrating your failures is an essential part of Failing Forward. By acknowledging and even celebrating your failures, you're reinforcing the idea that failure is a natural and necessary part of the journey. So, don't be afraid to throw a "Failure Party" every once in a while. It's

a KICKASS way to remind yourself that you're making progress, even when it doesn't feel like it.

7. Share Your Experiences: Sharing your failures with others can be a powerful and cathartic experience. Not only does it help you process your emotions and gain valuable insights, but it also inspires others to embrace the Art of Failing Forward. So, don't be afraid to open up about your setbacks – your story might just be the spark that ignites someone else's KICKASS journey.

In conclusion, mastering the Art of Failing Forward is a vital ingredient for a KICKASS life. By embracing your failures, learning from them, and using them as stepping stones to success, you're well on your way to a life filled with growth, accomplishment, and unbridled adventure. So, don't shy away from failure – face it head-on, learn from it, and watch as your life transforms into the KICKASS adventure you've always dreamed of.

Section 4: Living Life to the Fullest: Discovering true happiness through experiences, not material possessions, and embracing the present moment.

Hey there, KICKASS adventurer! It's time to dive into the secret sauce of living life to the absolute fullest. Forget about amassing material possessions and chasing shallow goals – true happiness lies in the richness of our experiences and the memories we create along the way. So, are you ready to uncover the path to a more meaningful, fulfilling life? Let's get started!

1. Experience Over Possessions: It's easy to get caught up in the never-ending race to accumulate more stuff, but material possessions can only provide temporary satisfaction. The real treasures in life are the experiences we share with the people we love and the memories we make together. So, trade that shiny new gadget for a weekend road trip with your friends or a once-in-a-lifetime journey to an exotic destination. Your future self will thank you for it.

2. Be Present and Mindful: Living life to the fullest means being fully present and engaged in every moment. Instead of constantly dwelling on the past or worrying about the future, practice mindfulness and focus on the here and now. Embrace every sensation, emotion, and experience as it comes, and you'll find that life becomes infinitely more vivid and fulfilling.

3. Forge Deep Connections: True happiness is often found in the company of others. Build strong, genuine connections with the people around you by being open, honest, and empathetic. Share your dreams, fears, and passions, and encourage others to do the same. These deep connections will not only enrich your life but also create a support network that will carry you through both the good times and the bad.

4. Find Your Purpose: To live life to the fullest, you need to find your true calling – the thing that sets your soul on fire and makes you feel alive. It could be your career, a

hobby, or a cause close to your heart. Whatever it is, pursue it with passion and dedication, and you'll find that life becomes an exhilarating journey of self-discovery and personal growth.

5. Take Care of Yourself: You can't live life to the fullest if you're constantly running on empty. Prioritize self-care by getting enough sleep, eating well, and engaging in regular physical activity. Don't forget to nurture your emotional and mental well-being too – practice gratitude, engage in activities that bring you joy, and take time to relax and recharge.

6. Face Your Fears: Fear can hold us back from truly living life to the fullest. Conquer your fears by confronting them head-on, one small step at a time. Each time you face a fear and emerge victorious, you'll gain confidence, strength, and a newfound appreciation for the KICKASS life you're living.

7. Give Back: Living life to the fullest isn't just about what you can gain; it's also about what you can give. Look for ways to make a positive impact in your community and the world at large. Volunteer, donate, or simply lend a helping hand to someone in need. By giving back, you'll not only enrich your own life but also make the world a better place for everyone.

In conclusion, living life to the fullest is about embracing every moment, forging deep connections, and pursuing your passions with relentless enthusiasm. So, go forth, KICKASS adventurer, and make your life a breathtaking mosaic of unforgettable experiences, heartfelt relationships, and meaningful accomplishments. The world is your oyster – savor every last drop of its KICKASS goodness!

Kickass Bonus Content: The 30-Day Adventure Challenge

Transform your life by embracing adventure with this 30-Day Adventure Challenge. Each day, choose one small action that pushes you out of your comfort zone or introduces you to a new experience. Examples include:

- Trying a new food
- Learning a new skill or hobby
- Reaching out to an old friend
- Going on a spontaneous day trip

At the end of the 30 days, reflect on the impact these small adventures have had on your life and happiness.

Chapter 4 Summary: Embracing the Thrill of the Unknown

In this chapter, we explored the adventure mindset, jumping off the comfort cliff, the art of failing forward, and living life to the fullest. By embracing these concepts, you can transform your life into a thrilling journey of personal growth, meaningful experiences, and lasting happiness.

Five KICKASS Questions to Reflect on:

1. How can you cultivate an adventure mindset in your daily life?

2. What steps can you take to push yourself out of your comfort zone and embrace the thrill of the unknown?

3. How have your past failures contributed to your personal growth, and how can you apply the concept of failing forward in the future?

4. In what ways can you prioritize experiences over material possessions to live a more fulfilling life?

5. Are you ready to take on the 30-Day Adventure Challenge, and how do you think it will impact your life and happiness?

Chapter 5: The Pursuit of Genuine Happiness

Section 1: Defining Happiness: Debunking myths about happiness and understanding what it truly means to be happy.

"True KICKASS happiness comes from appreciating what you have, not from constantly chasing what you don't." – Mickey T

Welcome to the KICKASS world of genuine happiness! Happiness is not about rainbows, unicorns, or endless success. It's not about money, fame, or getting every single thing you desire. It's about finding a deep sense of satisfaction and contentment with life - and that's what we're going to explore in this section.

But first, let's debunk some of the myths that have been clouding our understanding of happiness.

Myth 1: Happiness is all about material possessions Many people think that the key to happiness lies in acquiring more stuff - a bigger house, a better car, the latest gadgets. But research has shown that, beyond a certain point, material possessions don't contribute much to our happiness. In fact, constantly chasing after material things can leave us feeling empty and unfulfilled. True happiness comes from within - from our relationships, experiences, and personal growth.

Myth 2: Happiness is a destination The idea that we can achieve lasting happiness by reaching a specific goal or milestone is a common misconception. But the truth is, happiness is a journey, not a destination. Life is full of ups and downs, and we need to learn to find happiness in the present moment, regardless of our circumstances. The happiest people are those who can enjoy the ride, rather than obsessing over the destination.

Myth 3: Happy people never feel sad or stressed This is another big fat lie. Even the happiest people experience sadness, stress, and other negative emotions - it's all part of being human. But what sets genuinely happy people apart is their ability to bounce back from these emotions and maintain an overall positive outlook on life.

Now that we've debunked some of the biggest happiness myths, let's dive into what it truly means to be happy.

Happiness is a deeply personal and subjective experience, but there are some universal factors that contribute to our sense of well-being. Here are a few key elements of true happiness:

1. Authenticity: Being true to yourself and living a life that aligns with your values and passions is crucial to achieving genuine happiness. Don't try to please others or conform to society's expectations - be your own KICKASS self!

2. Connection: Strong, meaningful relationships with friends and family are the backbone of a happy life. Surround yourself with people who uplift and support you, and invest time and energy in nurturing these relationships.

3. Purpose: Having a sense of purpose and meaning in your life can provide a strong foundation for happiness.

Whether it's through your career, hobbies, or volunteering, find something that you're passionate about and make a positive impact on the world.

4. Resilience: Life is full of challenges and setbacks, but the ability to bounce back from adversity and maintain a positive outlook is key to lasting happiness. Cultivate resilience by practicing gratitude, focusing on your strengths, and seeking support from your social network.

5. Mindfulness: Being present and fully engaged in the moment - rather than constantly dwelling on the past or worrying about the future - can help you find greater happiness and satisfaction in life.

So, what does KICKASS happiness look like for you? It's time to take a deep dive into your own life and start cultivating the habits and mindset that will help you achieve genuine, lasting happiness. Stay tuned for the next section, where we'll explore the power of gratitude and how it can elevate your happiness levels to new heights!

Section 2: The Gratitude Attitude: Harnessing the power of gratitude to elevate your happiness levels.

"An attitude of gratitude is the KICKASS ingredient that adds flavor and richness to a happy life." – Mickey T

Are you ready to level up your happiness game? It's time to dive into the world of gratitude - a KICKASS attitude that can transform your life in ways you never imagined.

Gratitude is the practice of recognizing and appreciating the positive aspects of your life, no matter how small or insignificant they may seem. It's about focusing on the good things and acknowledging the people, experiences, and circumstances that contribute to your well-being.

Here's why cultivating a gratitude attitude is so powerful:

1. Gratitude rewires your brain: Studies have shown that practicing gratitude can actually change the neural pathways in your brain, making it easier for you to focus on the positive aspects of your life and increasing your overall sense of well-being.

2. Gratitude boosts happiness: When you focus on what you're grateful for, you're more likely to experience positive emotions, such as joy, love, and contentment, which can increase your overall happiness levels.

3. Gratitude strengthens relationships: Expressing gratitude towards others can deepen your connections, improve your communication, and create a more supportive and nurturing social network.

4. Gratitude reduces stress: By focusing on the good things in your life, you're less likely to get caught up in negativity and stress, allowing you to maintain a more balanced and peaceful state of mind.

So, how can you harness the power of gratitude and turn it into a KICKASS habit? Here are some simple exercises to help you get started:

A. Keep a gratitude journal: Dedicate a few minutes each day to writing down three things you're grateful for. It can be anything from a delicious meal to a supportive friend. The key is to be specific and consistent in your practice.

B. Gratitude letters: Write a heartfelt letter to someone who has made a significant impact on your life. Let them know how much you appreciate their presence and the difference they've made in your world.

C. Gratitude jar: Create a gratitude jar where you and your loved ones can drop notes of appreciation for each other. Make it a habit to read the notes together once a week or at the end of the month to strengthen your bonds and boost your collective happiness.

D. Gratitude meditation: Spend a few minutes each day focusing on your breath and visualizing the things you're grateful for. This can help you cultivate a deeper sense of appreciation and mindfulness.

E. Share your gratitude: Make it a habit to express gratitude regularly to the people around you. Let them know how much you appreciate their actions, words, or presence in your life.

By incorporating gratitude into your daily routine, you'll be on your way to a happier, more fulfilled life. So, what are you waiting for? Embrace the KICKASS power of gratitude and elevate your happiness levels like never before!

Section 3: The Ultimate Guide to Self-Care: Prioritizing mental, emotional, and physical well-being in the quest for happiness.

"Take care of your body. It's the only place you have to live." - Jim Rohn

KICKASS happiness starts with taking care of yourself, inside and out. Practicing self-care is a crucial part of maintaining mental, emotional, and physical well-being. It's not just about bubble baths and spa days (though those can be fun, too) - it's about nurturing yourself in a holistic way that allows you to show up as your best self every day. In this section, we'll provide the ultimate guide to self-care, packed with tips and strategies to help you prioritize your well-being and create a KICKASS self-care routine.

1. Mental self-care: Nourishing your mind is just as important as taking care of your body. Here are some ways to support your mental well-being:

- Engage in activities that challenge your brain, like puzzles, learning a new skill, or reading a thought-provoking book.

- Practice mindfulness through meditation, deep breathing exercises, or journaling.

- Set healthy boundaries by saying "no" when you need to and avoiding toxic relationships or situations.

- Prioritize sleep, as it's crucial for cognitive function and overall mental health.

2. Emotional self-care: Building emotional resilience and managing stress are essential for KICKASS happiness. Here's how to care for your emotional well-being:

- Allow yourself to feel your emotions, both positive and negative, without judgment.
- Seek support from friends, family, or a therapist when needed.
- Develop healthy coping strategies, like practicing gratitude, engaging in creative activities, or spending time in nature.
- Laugh often, as it can be an effective stress-reliever and mood booster.

3. Physical self-care: A healthy body is a happy body. Prioritize your physical health with these KICKASS self-care tips:

- Exercise regularly, aiming for a mix of cardiovascular, strength, and flexibility training.
- Fuel your body with nutrient-dense, whole foods that give you energy and support overall health.
- Stay hydrated by drinking plenty of water throughout the day.
- Schedule regular check-ups and preventive care with your healthcare provider.

4. Social self-care: Strong connections with others are essential for happiness, so don't neglect your social well-being:

- Make time for friends and family, whether it's through regular phone calls, video chats, or in-person get-togethers.

- Build a supportive network by seeking out like-minded individuals and joining clubs or groups that align with your interests.

- Practice active listening and empathy to strengthen your relationships and foster deeper connections.

5. Spiritual self-care: Nurturing your soul can help you find inner peace and happiness. Here are some ways to care for your spiritual well-being:

- Engage in activities that connect you with a sense of purpose, such as volunteering or participating in a religious or spiritual community.

- Practice mindfulness and meditation to cultivate inner calm and self-awareness.

- Spend time in nature, as it can be a powerful source of spiritual nourishment.

Remember, self-care is not selfish. In fact, it's the foundation for KICKASS happiness. So, prioritize your mental, emotional, and physical well-being, and watch as your happiness levels soar to new heights. Up next, we'll explore the Ripple Effect and how spreading positivity and kindness can create a cycle of happiness for you and others!

Section 4: The Ripple Effect: How spreading positivity and kindness can create a cycle of happiness for you and others.

"Be a KICKASS happiness warrior, and let your positivity create ripples that change the world." – Mickey T

You've heard the saying, "A rising tide lifts all boats," right? The same holds true for happiness. When you spread positivity and kindness, it creates a ripple effect that can impact the lives of countless people. In this KICKASS section, we're going to explore the power of the ripple effect and how you can use it to create a cycle of happiness for yourself and others.

1. Pay it forward One of the most powerful ways to create a ripple effect of happiness is to pay it forward. When someone does something kind for you, instead of just saying thank you, try to pass that kindness on to someone else. This creates a chain reaction of good deeds that can make a big impact on the world.

Here's an example of a KICKASS pay-it-forward exercise:

- When you get your morning coffee, pay for the person behind you in line.
- They might be inspired to pay for someone else's coffee or do another kind act later in the day.
- This can continue on and on, creating a ripple effect of kindness and happiness.

2. Share positivity Sharing positive news, quotes, and stories can be a powerful way to spread happiness and uplift others. In a world where negativity often dominates the headlines, being a beacon of positivity can make a significant difference.

Try this KICKASS challenge:

- For the next 30 days, share one positive story or quote on your social media every day.
- Encourage your friends and followers to do the same.
- Watch as the ripple effect of positivity spreads throughout your network.

3. Be kind to yourself The ripple effect starts with you. If you're not kind to yourself, it's hard to be kind to others. Make self-care and self-compassion a priority in your life, and watch as your newfound happiness radiates out to those around you.

Here's a KICKASS self-care exercise to try:

- Every night before bed, write down three things you did well that day or three things you're grateful for.
- This simple practice can help you cultivate self-compassion and a positive mindset.

4. Cultivate empathy and understanding When we practice empathy and understanding toward others, we're more likely to respond with kindness and compassion. This

not only helps us build stronger relationships but also creates a cycle of happiness that can spread far and wide.

A KICKASS empathy exercise:

- When you encounter someone who's upset or angry, take a moment to put yourself in their shoes and try to understand what they might be going through.

- Respond with kindness and understanding, even if it's difficult. You might just turn their day around and inspire them to pass the kindness on.

5. Practice random acts of kindness Random acts of kindness can create powerful ripples of happiness in the world. Look for opportunities to be kind and generous to others, even if it's something as small as holding the door or giving a sincere compliment.

Challenge yourself with this KICKASS kindness mission:

- Commit to performing one random act of kindness every day for a month.

- You might just be surprised by the impact your actions have on your own happiness and the happiness of those around you.

In conclusion, the ripple effect of happiness is a powerful force that can create lasting change in the world. By practicing kindness, positivity, and empathy, you can set off a chain reaction of joy that uplifts and inspires everyone it touches. So, go out there and be a KICKASS happiness warrior, spreading joy and positivity wherever you go. Remember, even the smallest acts of kindness can have a profound impact on those around you. And as you create a ripple effect of happiness, you'll also be nurturing your own well-being and personal growth.

So, let's recap the KICKASS ways to create a ripple effect of happiness:

1. Pay it forward: When someone does something kind for you, pass that kindness on to someone else, creating a chain reaction of good deeds.

2. Share positivity: For the next 30 days, share one positive story or quote on your social media every day, and encourage others to do the same.

3. Be kind to yourself: Practice self-care and self-compassion, nurturing your own happiness and well-being.

4. Cultivate empathy and understanding: Put yourself in others' shoes and respond with kindness and understanding, even in difficult situations.

5. Practice random acts of kindness: Commit to performing one random act of kindness every day for a month, and see the impact it has on your own happiness and the happiness of those around you.

By embracing these KICKASS practices, you'll not only improve your own happiness but also spread joy and positivity to others. You'll be a force of positive change, inspiring those around you to join the happiness movement. Together, we can create a world where happiness ripples outwards, touching the lives of countless people and making our world a better, brighter, and more KICKASS place to live.

Now, go forth and be the KICKASS happiness warrior you were born to be! With positivity and kindness as your weapons, you can change the world, one ripple at a time.

KICKASS Bonus Content: 5 Happiness-Boosting Activities to Try Today

1. Smile and say hello to strangers: Simple acts of friendliness can make someone's day and boost your own mood too. Make it a habit to smile and greet people you encounter throughout your day.

2. Write a heartfelt note or email: Take a moment to express your gratitude or appreciation to someone you care about. A heartfelt note can make a lasting impact and strengthen your connection.

3. Perform a stealth act of kindness: Do something kind for someone without them knowing it was you. This secret act of kindness can bring you a sense of joy and satisfaction that lasts all day.

4. Start a gratitude jar: Every day, write down something you're grateful for and place it in a jar. Over time, you'll

create a tangible reminder of all the good things in your life.

5. Dance it out: When you're feeling down, put on your favorite upbeat music and dance like nobody's watching. This fun, physical activity can instantly boost your mood and help you shake off stress.

Take your happiness to the next level with this 21-Day Happiness Challenge. Each day, commit to one action that promotes happiness and well-being in your life. Examples include:

- Sharing a genuine compliment with someone
- Spending time in nature
- Practicing mindfulness or meditation
- Engaging in a random act of kindness

At the end of the 21 days, reflect on the impact these actions have had on your overall happiness and well-being.

Chapter 5 Summary: The Pursuit of Genuine Happiness

In this KICKASS chapter, we explored the true meaning of happiness and debunked common myths about what it takes to be happy. We delved into the importance of gratitude, self-care, and spreading positivity to create a cycle of happiness for ourselves and others. Remember, happiness is not a destination, but a journey - and you have the power to create lasting, genuine happiness in your life.

Five KICKASS Questions to Reflect on:

1. What does genuine happiness look like for you, and how does it differ from the myths we debunked in this chapter?

2. How can you cultivate more gratitude in your daily life and create a lasting gratitude practice?

3. What self-care activities can you incorporate into your routine to prioritize your mental, emotional, and physical well-being?

4. How can you use the ripple effect to spread positivity and kindness in your community, both online and offline?

5. Reflect on the bonus content: Which of the KICKASS happiness-boosting activities resonate with you the most, and how can you make them a regular part of your life?

Take the time to thoughtfully answer these questions and put the lessons from this chapter into practice. Remember, happiness is within your reach - you just need to make a KICKASS effort to cultivate it in your life.

Chapter 6: Fearlessly Facing Change

Section 1: Embracing Life's Curveballs: Why change is inevitable and how to navigate it with grace and resilience.

Let me tell you something right off the bat: change is as inevitable as Monday mornings, and it's time we started treating it like a friend, not an enemy. So buckle up, because we're about to dive into the wild world of life's curveballs and learn how to knock 'em out of the park with style, resilience, and a KICKASS attitude.

You see, change is an essential part of life. It's a natural process that occurs whether we like it or not. Just like the seasons, life goes through cycles of growth, transformation, and renewal. It's time we stopped fighting change and started embracing it like a long-lost pal.

Why? Because life's curveballs are what make us stronger, wiser, and more adaptable. They push us out of our comfort zones, challenging us to rise above our fears and limitations. When we learn to navigate change with grace and resilience, we discover new opportunities, find inner strength, and ultimately become better, more badass versions of ourselves.

Here's a quote to get us started, from the legendary Bruce Lee: "Do not be assertive, but adjust to the object, and you shall find a way around or through it. If nothing within you stays rigid, outward things will disclose themselves."

So how do we start embracing life's curveballs? Let's break it down into some actionable steps:

1. Recognize that change is unavoidable: Stop resisting change and accept that it's a natural part of life. Remind yourself that every person, no matter how successful, has faced changes and challenges. You are not alone in this.

2. Adopt a flexible mindset: Be open to new ideas, experiences, and ways of thinking. This will help you adapt to change more quickly and minimize the stress and anxiety that can come from uncertainty. Remember, the more you bend, the less likely you are to break.

3. Keep your eyes on the prize: Focus on your long-term goals and dreams, but be prepared to take detours along the way. Sometimes, the most exciting adventures and opportunities arise when we least expect them.

4. Stay proactive: Don't just sit around waiting for change to happen. Be the captain of your ship and take charge of your life. Identify areas where you can grow, and actively seek out new experiences and challenges. This will make you more resilient and better equipped to handle change when it comes.

5. Learn from your past experiences: Reflect on the changes you've faced in the past and identify any lessons you can apply to your current situation. This will help you build resilience and develop a KICKASS attitude towards life's curveballs.

6. Cultivate a support network: Surround yourself with positive, like-minded people who can offer encouragement, advice, and a shoulder to lean on when the going gets tough. Your support network can be a powerful tool in helping you navigate change with grace and resilience.

Now, to make things more interactive, here's an exercise for you: Write down a list of changes you've faced in the past and how you dealt with them. Next, identify any patterns or strategies that helped you succeed, and consider how you can apply these lessons to future challenges.

Remember, life's curveballs are inevitable, but how you react to them is entirely up to you. By embracing change and adopting a KICKASS attitude, you can navigate life's twists and turns with grace, resilience, and an unbreakable spirit. So go ahead, hit those curveballs out of the park, and show the world what you're made of!

Section 2: The Silver Lining: Finding the opportunities in change and using them to grow and evolve.

Section 2: The Silver Lining: Finding the Opportunities in Change and Using Them to Grow and Evolve

Life is a rollercoaster, and change is the heart-pounding, adrenaline-pumping drop that makes the ride worth it. It's KICKASS, it's intense, and it can be downright terrifying. But guess what? You're not here for a dull, monotonous journey. You're here to grow, evolve, and unleash your inner badass. So let's talk about how you can find the silver lining in change and transform it into fuel for your personal growth.

First things first, let's get this out of the way: Change is inevitable. It's going to happen, whether you like it or not. What's crucial is how you react to it. When you're confronted with change, you can either run and hide or face it head-on like the KICKASS individual you are. The choice is yours.

To make the most out of change, you need to become an opportunity hunter. When life throws you curveballs, you've got to search for the hidden gems that lie within. Think of it as a treasure hunt for growth and self-improvement. Here are some tips to help you become an expert opportunity hunter:

1. Embrace the uncertainty: Sure, the unknown can be scary as hell, but it's also the breeding ground for new possibilities. When change comes knocking, open the door with open arms and a curious mind. Remember, change is the catalyst for growth, so embrace it wholeheartedly.

2. Adopt a "what if" mentality: Instead of dwelling on the potential downsides of change, shift your focus to the potential upsides. Ask yourself, "What if this change leads to something incredible?" When you start to view change through a more positive lens, you'll be better equipped to find the opportunities hidden within.

3. Connect with your inner badass: You've got a KICKASS spirit within you that's just waiting to be unleashed.

When confronted with change, channel your inner warrior and remind yourself of your strength, resilience, and adaptability. You've faced challenges before, and you've always come out stronger on the other side.

4. Look for the lessons: Every change, no matter how big or small, comes with a lesson (or several) attached. Be a student of life and seek out the teachings that change has to offer. When you actively search for the lessons in change, you'll uncover valuable insights that can propel you forward on your personal growth journey.

5. Stay flexible: Adaptability is the name of the game when it comes to thriving in the face of change. Keep your mind open and be willing to pivot as needed. The more flexible you are, the better equipped you'll be to seize the opportunities that change presents.

Now, to help you put these tips into practice, here's a KICKASS exercise for you:

The Silver Lining Exercise:

1. Think of a significant change you've experienced in your life. It could be a job loss, a breakup, a move, or any other event that shook up your world.

2. Write down any negative emotions or thoughts you had at the time. Be honest with yourself and let it all out.

3. Now, with your newfound opportunity hunting skills, look back on that change and search for the silver lining.

What lessons did you learn? What growth opportunities did you uncover? What new possibilities emerged because of that change?

4. Write down your findings and reflect on how that change ultimately led to growth and evolution.

Remember, my friend, change is a KICKASS force for growth and evolution. It may be challenging at times and even downright uncomfortable, but it's a necessary part of life that propels us forward. So, when change comes knocking, don't shy away from it. Embrace it, find the silver lining, and use it as an opportunity to grow, evolve, and become the best version of yourself. After all, you're a KICKASS individual who's capable of tackling anything life throws your way. Keep chasing those opportunities, and remember: fortune favors the bold.

Section 3: The Growth Mindset: Adopting a mindset that welcomes change and cultivates personal growth.

You know what's truly KICKASS? Having a growth mindset. It's the secret sauce that separates the go-getters from the naysayers, the ones who thrive in the face of change from those who crumble under pressure. But what exactly is a growth mindset, and how can you cultivate it in your own life? Buckle up, because we're about to dive deep into this game-changing mentality.

A growth mindset is a belief that your abilities and intelligence can be developed and improved through hard work, dedication, and learning from experiences. It's the antithesis of a fixed mindset, which assumes that our qualities are set in stone and can't be changed. With a growth mindset, you're not afraid of change – you embrace it as an opportunity to become a better version of yourself.

So how do you adopt a growth mindset and become a master of personal growth? Here are some KICKASS strategies to get you started:

1. Embrace challenges: Challenges are the ultimate growth opportunities. Instead of shying away from them, face them head-on, and see them as a chance to learn, grow, and push your limits. When you view challenges as a necessary part of your personal growth journey, you'll be more likely to tackle them with enthusiasm and determination.

2. Learn from failure: Failure is not a dead-end; it's a stepping stone on your path to success. When you experience setbacks or disappointments, don't beat yourself up. Instead, examine the situation, figure out what went wrong, and use that knowledge to improve and avoid making the same mistakes in the future.

3. Practice persistence: Rome wasn't built in a day, and neither will your growth mindset. It takes time, patience, and persistence to cultivate this powerful mentality. So, when the going gets tough, don't give up – keep pushing forward, and remind yourself that every step you take, no matter how small, brings you closer to your goals.

4. Seek out feedback: We can't grow in a vacuum. Constructive criticism and feedback from others can provide valuable insights into areas where we can improve. Don't be afraid to ask for feedback and take it to heart – use it as fuel to propel your personal growth journey forward.

5. Surround yourself with like-minded individuals: Your environment plays a significant role in shaping your mindset. Surround yourself with people who share your passion for growth and self-improvement. Their positive energy and encouragement will help keep you motivated and inspired to keep pushing forward.

Ready for a KICKASS exercise to help you cultivate a growth mindset? Let's do this:

The Growth Mindset Exercise:

1. Identify an area of your life where you'd like to improve or grow. It could be related to your career, relationships, health, or any other aspect that's important to you.

2. Write down any fixed mindset thoughts or beliefs you might have about this area. Be brutally honest with yourself – these beliefs could be holding you back from reaching your full potential.

3. Now, transform those fixed mindset thoughts into growth mindset statements. For example, if your fixed mindset thought is "I'm just not good at public speaking," turn it into a growth mindset statement like "I

can improve my public speaking skills with practice and effort."

4. Create an action plan for growth in that area. Outline the steps you'll take to work on your skills, learn from your experiences, and overcome obstacles.

5. Keep a journal to track your progress and celebrate your successes along the way.

Embrace the growth mindset, my friend, and you'll unlock a world of possibilities for personal growth and self-improvement. With this powerful mentality in your arsenal, you'll be better equipped to face change, overcome challenges, and make the most of every opportunity that comes your way. So go forth, cultivate that growth mindset, and become the KICKASS individual you're destined to be. Remember, the sky's the limit when you believe in your ability to grow and evolve.

Section 4: Bouncing Back: How to recover from setbacks and turn them into comebacks.

Let's face it: life can be a real kick in the teeth sometimes. Setbacks happen, and they can be tough to swallow. But you know what's even more KICKASS than never experiencing setbacks? Bouncing back from them like a f*cking champion. Because guess what? Resilience is the ultimate superpower, and it's yours for the taking.

Here are some KICKASS strategies to help you bounce back from setbacks and turn them into epic comebacks:

1. Accept the situation: Denial might feel comforting, but it won't get you anywhere. Acknowledge the setback, embrace the emotions that come with it, and then make a conscious decision to move forward. Remember, the faster you accept the situation, the quicker you can start working on your comeback.

2. Reframe your perspective: A setback is only a failure if you allow it to be. Instead, choose to see it as an opportunity for growth, learning, and self-improvement. Reframe your perspective and remind yourself that every setback is a stepping stone on your journey to success.

3. Build a support network: You don't have to go through tough times alone. Reach out to friends, family, or mentors who can offer guidance, encouragement, and a shoulder to lean on. Having a support network will not only help you bounce back faster but also remind you that you're not alone in this journey.

4. Focus on what you can control: Setbacks often leave us feeling helpless, but it's crucial to remember that there are still aspects of your life that you can control. Focus on those areas and channel your energy into taking positive action. This will help you regain a sense of control and boost your self-confidence.

5. Develop a plan of action: Now that you've accepted the situation and focused on what you can control, it's time to create a plan of action. Break down your goals into

manageable steps, and start working towards them one day at a time. Remember, progress is progress, no matter how small.

Ready to put these strategies into action? Here's a KICKASS exercise to help you bounce back from setbacks:

The Bounce Back Exercise:

1. Reflect on a recent setback you've experienced. It could be anything from a failed project to a personal loss.

2. Write down the emotions and thoughts you felt during that time. Be honest and allow yourself to feel those emotions fully.

3. Now, use the strategies listed above to reframe your perspective, accept the situation, and develop a plan of action for moving forward.

4. Set short-term and long-term goals related to your comeback, and keep track of your progress in a journal.

5. Celebrate your successes along the way, and remember that setbacks are temporary – you have the power to turn them into comebacks.

Bouncing back from setbacks might not be easy, but with determination, resilience, and a KICKASS attitude, you'll be well on your way to transforming those setbacks into epic comebacks. So, bring it on, life – you've got this!

By embracing life's curveballs, finding the silver lining, adopting a growth mindset, and bouncing back from setbacks, you can fearlessly face change and continue to live life, do good, and be happy, no matter what challenges come your way.

KICKASS Bonus Content: The 5-Step Personal Growth Challenge

Ready to put everything you've learned in Chapter 6 into action? Then it's time to take on the KICKASS 5-Step Personal Growth Challenge! This challenge is designed to help you fearlessly face change, uncover the silver linings, cultivate a growth mindset, and bounce back from setbacks like a champ.

Here's how it works:

1. For the next 30 days, commit to completing one task or activity each day that pushes you out of your comfort zone and helps you grow as an individual.

2. Document your journey in a journal, noting the challenges you faced, the lessons you learned, and the progress you made.

3. Share your experiences with your support network, and encourage them to join you in the challenge.

4. At the end of the 30 days, reflect on your journey and celebrate your growth and achievements.

5. Keep the momentum going! Use the insights and experiences from the challenge to set new personal

growth goals and continue evolving as a KICKASS individual.

Now, let's wrap up Chapter 6 with a summary and some thought-provoking questions.

Chapter 6 Summary:

In this chapter, we explored the art of fearlessly facing change by:

1. Embracing life's curveballs and learning to navigate them with grace and resilience.

2. Finding the silver lining in change and using it to grow and evolve.

3. Adopting a growth mindset that welcomes change and cultivates personal growth.

4. Bouncing back from setbacks and turning them into comebacks.

Five KICKASS Questions to Reflect on:

1. How have you handled change in the past? What can you do differently moving forward to make the most of the opportunities that come with change?

2. Can you think of a recent challenge or setback you've faced? What was the silver lining, and how did it contribute to your personal growth?

3. In what areas of your life do you feel you have a fixed mindset? How can you work on transforming those beliefs into a growth mindset?

4. Share a story of a time when you bounced back from a setback and turned it into a comeback. What strategies or tools did you use to help you succeed?

5. Are you ready to take on the KICKASS 5-Step Personal Growth Challenge? What do you hope to gain from the experience, and how will it help you become a more resilient, adaptable, and fearless individual?

With these insights and tools under your belt, you're ready to tackle whatever changes life throws your way. Embrace the uncertainty, find the opportunities within, and always remember that you're a KICKASS individual who can rise above any challenge.

Chapter 7: Daring to Dream Big

1. The Power of Vision: How to set audacious goals and create a roadmap to achieve them.

KICKASS! Let's get started.

When it comes to setting goals, we often play it safe. We think small and settle for mediocrity. But it's time to change that. It's time to dare to dream big and unleash your true potential. In this section, we'll explore the power of vision, and how to set audacious goals that will inspire you and drive you to achieve them. Buckle up, because we're about to kick some serious ass.

"Your vision will become clear only when you look into your heart. Who looks outside, dreams. Who looks inside, awakens." - Carl Jung

Now, let's break it down step by step.

1. Dream Big: If you want to achieve greatness, you have to think big. Don't be afraid to let your imagination run wild and envision the life you truly desire. Remember, if your dreams don't scare you, they're not big enough.

Exercise. Take a moment to visualize your perfect day. What would it look like? Who would be with you? What would you be doing? Be specific and let your mind wander.

2. Set Audacious Goals: Once you've dared to dream big, it's time to set some audacious goals. These should be goals that push you out of your comfort zone and force

you to grow. They should be KICKASS and exciting, so much so that you can't wait to start working on them.

Exercise: Write down at least three audacious goals that align with your dream life. Remember to make them SMART (Specific, Measurable, Achievable, Relevant, and Time-bound).

3. Create a Roadmap: You've got your goals, but how do you make them a reality? It's time to create a roadmap that outlines the steps you need to take to achieve each goal. Break down your goals into smaller, more manageable tasks, and assign deadlines to each. This will help you stay on track and motivated.

Exercise: For each of your audacious goals, create a list of smaller tasks that need to be completed in order to achieve the goal. Assign deadlines to each task, and make a note of any resources or support you'll need along the way.

4. Track Your Progress: As you work towards your goals, it's essential to track your progress. This will help you stay focused, motivated, and accountable. Plus, it's super satisfying to check things off your list as you accomplish them!

Exercise: Create a system for tracking your progress. This could be a physical planner, an app on your phone, or a simple spreadsheet. Choose a method that works for you and update it regularly.

5. Celebrate Your Successes: When you achieve a milestone or reach one of your goals, take the time to

celebrate. This will help reinforce your positive behaviors and build momentum as you work towards your next goal.

Exercise: Plan a celebration for each of your audacious goals. It could be a trip, a fancy dinner, or just a day off to relax and enjoy your success. Whatever it is, make sure it's something that excites and motivates you.

Remember, the journey to achieving your audacious goals won't always be smooth sailing. There will be obstacles, setbacks, and moments of self-doubt. But as long as you keep your vision alive and stay committed to your roadmap, you'll be unstoppable.

So, what are you waiting for? Dare to dream big and harness the power of vision to create a KICKASS life that you're truly passionate about. And always remember, "You are the architect of your own destiny. Your dreams, your vision, and your KICKASS goals are the blueprint for your future. So, get out there, take action, and make it happen!"

Now that you've got the power of vision on your side, you're ready to tackle the next challenge — overcoming self-doubt. Stay tuned for the next section, where we'll delve into strategies to silence your inner critic and unleash your full potential. Let's keep this KICKASS journey going!

2. Overcoming Self-Doubt: Strategies to silence your inner critic and unleash your full potential.

You've dared to dream big, set audacious goals, and created a roadmap to achieve them. But now, it's time to face your greatest enemy – your own self-doubt. This inner critic can be relentless, tearing down your confidence and undermining your progress. But fear not! We've got some KICKASS strategies to help you silence that pesky voice and unleash your full potential.

"Believe in yourself and all that you are. Know that there is something inside you that is greater than any obstacle." – Christian D. Larson

Let's dive in and crush self-doubt once and for all.

1. Recognize and Challenge Negative Thoughts: The first step in overcoming self-doubt is to recognize when your inner critic is speaking. When negative thoughts arise, challenge them by asking, "Is this really true?" or "What evidence do I have to support this belief?" More often than not, you'll find that your self-doubt is based on unfounded fears and irrational thoughts.

Exercise: Keep a journal to track your negative thoughts. When you notice a pattern, challenge those beliefs and replace them with positive affirmations.

2. Surround Yourself with Positive Influences: It's crucial to surround yourself with people who believe in you and support your goals. Their encouragement and positive

energy will help drown out your inner critic and keep you focused on your KICKASS journey.

Exercise: Make a list of the people in your life who support and inspire you. Reach out to them regularly and share your progress, challenges, and successes.

3. Develop Your Skills and Knowledge: One way to silence self-doubt is to become more confident in your abilities. Invest time and energy into developing your skills and expanding your knowledge. This will not only boost your self-confidence but also make you more effective in achieving your goals.

Exercise: Identify areas where you'd like to improve or learn something new. Create a plan to develop these skills through courses, workshops, books, or online resources.

4. Embrace Failure as a Learning Opportunity: Failure is an inevitable part of life, but it doesn't have to be a roadblock. Instead, view it as a valuable learning experience that can help you grow and improve. When you embrace failure, you remove its power to fuel self-doubt.

Exercise: Reflect on a recent failure or setback. What lessons can you learn from it? How can you apply these insights to your future endeavors?

5. Practice Self-Compassion: Be kind to yourself and remember that everyone experiences self-doubt at

times. Treat yourself with the same compassion and understanding that you would offer to a friend in need.

Exercise: Write yourself a letter or have a conversation with yourself as if you were talking to a friend who's struggling with self-doubt. Offer support, encouragement, and advice on how to overcome it.

By implementing these KICKASS strategies, you'll be well on your way to overcoming self-doubt and unleashing your full potential. Now that you've got the tools to conquer your inner critic, you're ready to tackle the next section: The Art of Hustle. Let's keep this momentum going!

3. The Art of Hustle: Channeling your passion and drive into tangible results.

Welcome to the KICKASS world of hustle! In this section, we're going to explore how to channel your passion and drive into tangible results. You've dared to dream big and set audacious goals – now it's time to take action and make those dreams a reality. So, let's dive in and learn the art of hustle.

"Things may come to those who wait, but only the things left by those who hustle." - Abraham Lincoln

Here's how you can channel your passion and drive into tangible results:

1. Prioritize Your Goals: With so many things vying for your attention, it's essential to prioritize your goals. Focus on

the tasks and projects that align with your audacious goals and vision, and let the rest take a backseat.

Exercise: Rank your goals and projects based on their importance and urgency. Use this ranking to guide your daily, weekly, and monthly task lists.

2. Take Consistent Action: The key to achieving tangible results is to take consistent action. Make a commitment to work on your goals every single day, even if it's just for a short amount of time. Consistency is what separates the KICKASS hustlers from the wannabes.

Exercise: Set aside dedicated time each day to work on your goals. Establish a routine and stick to it – consistency is crucial!

3. Embrace the Grind: Hustle isn't always glamorous. It involves hard work, dedication, and sacrifice. Embrace the grind and remember that every challenge you face is an opportunity to grow and become stronger.

Exercise: Identify any obstacles or challenges you may face while working towards your goals. Develop a plan to overcome them and remind yourself that the grind is part of the journey.

4. Network Like a Pro: Networking is a powerful tool for turning your passion and drive into tangible results. Surround yourself with like-minded individuals who share your KICKASS ambition and can offer support, advice, and connections.

Exercise: Attend industry events, join online communities, and actively seek out networking opportunities. Don't be afraid to reach out and connect with others — you never know where it might lead.

5. Stay Adaptable: The path to success is rarely a straight line. Be prepared to pivot, adapt, and change course as needed. Keep an open mind and be willing to explore new opportunities and ideas.

Exercise: Regularly review your goals and progress, and be ready to make adjustments as necessary. Remember, flexibility is an essential component of the art of hustle.

By mastering the art of hustle, you'll be able to channel your passion and drive into tangible results, bringing you one step closer to your audacious goals and dream life. So, get out there, embrace the grind, and make some KICKASS things happen!

Stay tuned for the next section, where we'll explore the success mindset and how to develop a mindset that attracts success and happiness. The journey continues!

4. The Success Mindset: Developing a mindset that attracts success and happiness.

You've dared to dream big, set audacious goals, and started hustling. But there's one more crucial piece to the puzzle — developing a KICKASS success mindset. Your mindset can either propel you towards greatness or hold you back. In this section, we'll explore how to cultivate a mindset that attracts success and happiness. Let's dive in!

"Success is not the key to happiness. Happiness is the key to success. If you love what you are doing, you will be successful." - Albert Schweitzer

1. Embrace the Growth Mindset: The growth mindset is the belief that your abilities and intelligence can be developed through hard work, dedication, and persistence. Embrace the idea that failure is just an opportunity to learn and grow, and that setbacks are merely stepping stones on your journey to success.

Exercise: Identify a recent failure or setback. Reflect on what you learned from the experience and how you can use that knowledge to grow and improve.

2. Cultivate Gratitude: Gratitude is a powerful tool in creating a success mindset. By focusing on the positive aspects of your life and expressing gratitude for what you have, you'll attract more abundance and happiness.

Exercise: Every day, write down three things you're grateful for. They can be as simple or as significant as you want. This practice will help you stay grounded and maintain a positive outlook.

3. Develop Mental Toughness: Mental toughness is the ability to stay resilient and focused, even in the face of adversity. By building mental toughness, you'll be able to

push through challenges and maintain your drive towards success.

Exercise: Practice mindfulness techniques, such as meditation or deep breathing, to help you stay centered and focused during difficult moments.

4. Surround Yourself with Positive Influences: Your environment has a significant impact on your mindset. Surround yourself with people who support, inspire, and challenge you to be your best self.

Exercise: Evaluate your current social circle. Identify any toxic or negative influences, and distance yourself from them. Seek out new connections that align with your goals and values.

5. Believe in Yourself: Confidence is key to a success mindset. Believe in your abilities, trust your instincts, and have faith in your journey. Remember, you're capable of achieving greatness!

Exercise: Create a list of your strengths and accomplishments. Review this list regularly to remind yourself of your capabilities and boost your self-confidence.

By developing a KICKASS success mindset, you'll be able to overcome obstacles, maintain a positive outlook, and ultimately, attract the success and happiness you deserve. So, go forth with confidence and conquer your dreams! And always remember, "The only limit to our realization of tomorrow will be our doubts of today." - Franklin D. Roosevelt

KICKASS Bonus Content: 5 Mind-Blowing Quotes to Supercharge Your Success Mindset

1. "Do not wait; the time will never be 'just right.' Start where you stand, and work with whatever tools you may have at your command, and better tools will be found as you go along." - George Herbert

2. "The greatest glory in living lies not in never falling, but in rising every time we fall." - Nelson Mandela

3. "What lies behind us and what lies before us are tiny matters compared to what lies within us." - Ralph Waldo Emerson

4. "You miss 100% of the shots you don't take." - Wayne Gretzky

5. "The best way to predict the future is to create it." - Peter Drucker

Chapter 7 Summary: Daring to Dream Big

In this KICKASS chapter, we've explored the power of daring to dream big and how to:

1. Set audacious goals with a powerful vision.

2. Overcome self-doubt and silence your inner critic.

3. Harness the art of hustle and channel your passion into tangible results.

4. Develop a success mindset that attracts success and happiness.

By applying the strategies and techniques outlined in this chapter, you'll be well on your way to living a life that's not only extraordinary but truly KICKASS.

Five KICKASS Questions to Reflect on:

Now, let's wrap things up with five thought-provoking questions to help you reflect on your journey:

1. What's one audacious goal you've set for yourself after reading this chapter, and what steps will you take to achieve it?

2. How will you silence your inner critic and overcome self-doubt on your journey to success?

3. In what ways can you incorporate the art of hustle into your daily life to drive tangible results?

4. Which of the success mindset strategies resonates with you the most, and how do you plan to implement it?

5. How will you continue to cultivate a growth mindset and embrace challenges as opportunities for growth?

Keep these questions in mind as you embark on your journey to dream big and create a KICKASS life that you're passionate about. Remember, you have the power within you to achieve greatness. It's time to unleash it!

Chapter 8: Living Life, Doing Good, Being Happy

Section 1: The Ultimate Balance: How to create a life that balances passion, purpose, and happiness.

Let me kick this off with a KICKASS quote that'll fire you up: "You can't live a perfect day without doing something for someone who will never be able to repay you." - John Wooden. Now, let's dive into the Ultimate Balance, baby!

The Ultimate Balance is about finding harmony among three essential elements: passion, purpose, and happiness. It's about living a life that's not only personally fulfilling but also beneficial to others and the world around you. Here's the KICKASS guide to achieving that sweet spot of balance.

Step 1: Discover your passion

You've got to find that fire inside you, that thing that makes your heart race and your palms sweat. It's the fuel for your KICKASS life! Start by asking yourself these questions:

- What activities make me feel alive?
- If money were no object, what would I spend my time doing?
- Which causes, ideas, or values resonate with me the most?

Remember, it's all about finding what genuinely makes you happy and excited. Experiment, try new things, and give yourself permission to explore.

Step 2: Define your purpose

Your purpose is the "why" behind your passion. It's the reason you get up in the morning and the driving force behind your actions. To find your purpose, reflect on these questions:

- How can my passion make a positive impact on others or the world?
- What specific problems or challenges do I feel called to address?
- What unique talents or strengths can I use to make a difference?

Write your answers down and create a mission statement for your life, something that'll guide you in making decisions and staying true to your path.

Step 3: Cultivate happiness

Happiness isn't a destination, it's a journey. It's about choosing to live in a way that brings joy and fulfillment to yourself and others. Here are some KICKASS ways to cultivate happiness:

- Practice gratitude: Take time each day to reflect on what you're thankful for. It's a simple yet powerful way to shift your focus from what you don't have to what you do have.
- Build relationships: Connect with others, foster strong bonds, and prioritize your loved ones. Happiness is

contagious, and when you surround yourself with positive people, you'll find your happiness skyrocketing.

- Embrace failure: Don't be afraid to fail. Embrace setbacks as learning experiences and growth opportunities. Remember, no great success was ever achieved without a few bumps along the way.

Step 4: Create a balanced life

Now that you've got your passion, purpose, and happiness on lock, it's time to bring them all together. Here are some KICKASS tips to create a balanced life:

- Set goals: Break your big vision down into smaller, manageable objectives. This will help you stay focused and motivated as you work towards achieving your Ultimate Balance.

- Prioritize self-care: Make time for yourself, and prioritize your mental and physical well-being. Remember, you can't pour from an empty cup.

- Seek support: Surround yourself with like-minded people who share your values and ambitions. They'll be your cheerleaders, sounding boards, and accountability buddies on this KICKASS journey.

Now, you're ready to live a life of Ultimate Balance, one that's filled with passion, purpose, and happiness. You've got this! Just remember, in the wise words of the legendary Gary Vaynerchuk, "Ultimately, a value exchange matters the most.

No matter what, if you bring somebody value, if you make somebody laugh, if you make somebody think, if you deliver on your promise, that is always going to work out, no matter how you do that." and make this life absolutely KICKASS!

Section 2: The Power of Giving: Why doing good for others can bring immense happiness and fulfillment.

Alright, let's jump into the KICKASS world of giving! As the great Winston Churchill once said, "We make a living by what we get, but we make a life by what we give." So, let's dive into why giving is so powerful and how it can lead to a life of happiness and fulfillment.

1. Giving creates a sense of connection

When you give, you create a connection with the person you're helping. This connection is a two-way street, with both parties benefiting from the exchange. The giver experiences the joy of helping someone in need, while the receiver gains a sense of gratitude and appreciation. It's a win-win situation that fosters empathy, compassion, and understanding.

2. Giving boosts your self-esteem

When you do good for others, it naturally boosts your self-esteem. You start to see yourself as a KICKASS individual capable of making a positive impact in the world. This newfound confidence will spill over into other areas of your life, leading to more success and happiness.

3. Giving helps you grow

Helping others often pushes you out of your comfort zone, leading to personal growth and development. It challenges you to expand your skills, knowledge, and understanding. As you grow, you'll become more adaptable, resilient, and capable of handling whatever life throws your way.

4. Giving creates a cycle of good

When you give, it sets off a ripple effect of goodness. Your act of kindness inspires the receiver to pay it forward, which in turn inspires others. This cycle of giving creates a more compassionate, empathetic, and KICKASS world.

Now, let's dive into some practical ways to harness the power of giving:

1. Volunteer your time

Whether it's at a local food bank, animal shelter, or mentoring program, find a cause that resonates with you and dedicate some time to it. Not only will you be making a difference, but you'll also connect with like-minded individuals who share your passion for giving.

2. Donate to a cause

If you're short on time, consider making a financial contribution to a charity or cause that aligns with your values. No matter how big or small, your donation will make an impact.

3. Perform random acts of kindness

Look for opportunities to brighten someone's day, whether it's by complimenting a stranger, holding the door open for someone, or simply smiling at someone as you pass by. These small acts can have a profound impact on both the giver and the receiver.

4. Share your knowledge and skills

Are you an expert in a particular field or have a unique skill set? Share your knowledge and expertise with others who could benefit from it. Teach a class, mentor someone, or write articles or blog posts to share your wisdom.

Remember, giving is a KICKASS way to create a life of happiness and fulfillment. In the words of the legendary Muhammad Ali, "Service to others is the rent you pay for your room here on earth" and start making a difference in the world by harnessing the power of giving.

Section 3: Crafting Your Legacy: How to make a lasting impact on the world and leave it better than you found it.

Alright, it's time to build your KICKASS legacy! Your legacy is the mark you leave on the world and the impact you have on others. It's what people will remember about you long after you're gone. So, let's dive into some tips on how to craft a legacy that lasts.

1. Define your core values

Your core values are the guiding principles that shape your life and your legacy. Take some time to reflect on what matters most to you, and use these values as a compass to guide your actions and decisions. When your life is aligned with your core values, you're more likely to create a lasting impact that's true to who you are.

2. Set meaningful goals

To leave a lasting legacy, you need to set goals that are both ambitious and meaningful. These goals should align with your core values and have a positive impact on the world. Break these big goals down into smaller, actionable steps, and start working towards them one day at a time.

3. Be a role model

One of the most powerful ways to create a KICKASS legacy is by being a role model to others. Live your life with integrity, and lead by example. Inspire those around you with your actions, and show them what's possible when you live a life driven by passion, purpose, and happiness.

4. Make connections and build relationships

Your legacy is not just about what you do, but also about the people you touch along the way. Invest time in building strong relationships with others, and be a positive force in their lives. Support, encourage, and lift others up, and you'll create a lasting impact that ripples out into the world.

5. Give back

Generosity is a cornerstone of a lasting legacy. Look for ways to give back to your community and the world at large. This could be through volunteering, donating to a cause, or simply being there for someone in need. When you give, you create a cycle of good that continues long after you're gone.

6. Keep learning and growing

To create a KICKASS legacy, you must be committed to personal growth and continuous improvement. Seek out new experiences, challenge yourself, and learn from your failures. As you grow and evolve, so too will your legacy.

7. Share your story

Your story is unique and powerful. Share it with the world, and inspire others with your journey. Write a book, start a blog, or give talks about your experiences. Your story has the power to touch lives and create a lasting impact.

8. Identify your unique contributions

Next, think about what you're exceptionally good at or passionate about. What are your unique gifts and talents? How can you use these to make a difference in the world? By leveraging your strengths, you'll have a greater impact and be more likely to leave a lasting legacy.

9. Build strong relationships

Your legacy isn't just about what you do; it's also about who you impact. Build strong relationships with the people around you, and make a conscious effort to support, uplift, and inspire them. By fostering a network of connections, you'll create a ripple effect that extends far beyond your own actions.

10. Stay committed and consistent

Crafting a legacy is a long-term endeavor, and it requires dedication and persistence. Stay committed to your goals, even when you face obstacles or setbacks. Consistency is key, so keep pushing forward and stay true to your vision.

11. Reflect and adjust

As you work towards your legacy, take the time to reflect on your progress and make adjustments as needed. Are your actions aligned with your values and goals? Are you making the impact you desire? By regularly evaluating your progress, you'll stay focused and ensure you're on the right path.

12. Inspire others

Lastly, remember that your legacy isn't just about you; it's about inspiring others to carry on your work and make their own positive impact. Share your story, your successes, and your challenges, and be open to mentoring and supporting others on their journeys.

With these KICKASS steps, you'll be well on your way to crafting a legacy that leaves a lasting, positive impact on the world. So go forth, and create a legacy that not only makes you proud but also inspires future generations to continue making the world a better place.

Section 4: The Happiness Manifesto: A guide to living life to the fullest, doing good, and finding your path to happiness.

Get ready for the KICKASS Happiness Manifesto, your ultimate guide to living life to the fullest, doing good, and finding your path to happiness! As the inspiring Helen Keller once said, "Happiness cannot come from without. It must come from within." Let's dive right in:

1. Embrace your authentic self

Be true to who you are, and don't let society's expectations or norms dictate your choices. Embrace your quirks, your passions, and your unique perspective. When you live authentically, you'll find greater joy and satisfaction in everything you do.

Exercise: Create a list of your unique qualities, passions, and values. Keep this list somewhere visible as a reminder to stay true to yourself.

2. Cultivate a positive mindset

Your thoughts have a powerful impact on your happiness. Choose to focus on the positive, and practice gratitude for the blessings in your life. Surround yourself with uplifting, like-minded people, and create a supportive environment that fosters happiness and growth.

Exercise: Start a gratitude journal, and each day, write down three things you're grateful for.

3. Pursue your passions

Life is too short not to do what you love. Identify your passions and make time for them in your life. Whether it's a hobby, a career, or a cause you're passionate about, pursuing what sets your soul on fire will lead to a more fulfilling and happy life.

4. Nurture meaningful connections

Relationships are the cornerstone of happiness. Invest time and energy into building strong, supportive connections with family, friends, and loved ones. Be present, listen deeply, and show appreciation for the people who matter most.

Exercise: Schedule regular catch-ups with friends and family, and make an effort to connect with someone new each week.

5. Prioritize self-care

You can't pour from an empty cup, so prioritize self-care to maintain your mental, emotional, and physical well-being. Eat well, exercise regularly, get enough sleep, and practice stress-reducing activities like meditation, yoga, or spending time in nature.

6. Give back to others

As we discussed earlier, giving back to others is a powerful way to boost your happiness and sense of fulfillment. Look for opportunities to volunteer, donate, or simply perform random acts of kindness. When you focus on making the world a better place, you'll find happiness in the process.

7. Embrace life's journey

Life is full of ups and downs, but every challenge presents an opportunity for growth and learning. Embrace the journey, and be open to change and new experiences. Remember, happiness isn't a destination, but a lifelong pursuit.

Exercise: Reflect on a past challenge and identify what you learned from it. How can you apply this wisdom to your current situation or future endeavors?

8. Leave a positive impact

Finally, strive to leave a positive impact on the world. By crafting your legacy, as we explored in Section 3, you'll not only enrich your own life but also inspire others to pursue their own paths to happiness.

This KICKASS Happiness Manifesto, now enriched with quotes and exercises, is your roadmap to living life to the fullest, doing good, and finding your path to happiness. Keep these principles in mind as you navigate the ups and downs of life, and remember that happiness is an ongoing journey, not a final destination. As Ralph Waldo Emerson wisely said, "For every minute you are angry, you lose sixty seconds of happiness." Embrace the adventure, and live your life to the absolute fullest!

Bonus Content: The KICKASS Happiness Toolkit

Here's a little bonus for you — the KICKASS Happiness Toolkit! It's packed with extra resources and strategies to supercharge your happiness journey:

1. Inspirational Books: Build a library of uplifting and inspiring books to keep your motivation and positivity high. Some great reads include "The Happiness Advantage" by Shawn Achor, "The Power of Now" by Eckhart Tolle, and "Big Magic" by Elizabeth Gilbert.

2. Affirmations: Use positive affirmations to reinforce your happiness mindset. Write down a few powerful statements that resonate with you, and repeat them daily to rewire your brain for happiness.

3. TED Talks: Watch inspiring TED Talks on happiness and well-being to expand your knowledge and gain fresh insights. Some excellent talks to start with are "The Happy Secret to Better Work" by Shawn Achor and "The Surprising Science of Happiness" by Dan Gilbert.

4. Meditation Apps: Incorporate meditation into your daily routine to reduce stress and increase happiness. Check out apps like Headspace, Calm, or Insight Timer to find guided meditations suited to your needs and preferences.

5. Support Groups: Connect with like-minded individuals in online forums or local meetup groups dedicated to personal growth and happiness. Share your experiences, ask questions, and learn from the collective wisdom of the group.

Summary of Chapter 8: Living Life, Doing Good, Being Happy

In Chapter 8, we explored how to create a life that balances passion, purpose, and happiness. We discussed the power of giving and its impact on our well-being, learned how to craft a lasting legacy, and unveiled the Happiness Manifesto as a guide to living life to the fullest.

Five KICKASS Questions to Reflect on:

Reflect on your journey through this chapter by answering these five questions:

1. What are your core values, and how can they guide you in creating a balanced, happy life?

2. How can you give back to others in a meaningful way that aligns with your passions and skills?

3. What steps can you take to start crafting your legacy and make a positive impact on the world?

4. Which aspects of the Happiness Manifesto resonate most with you, and how will you incorporate them into your daily life?

5. What additional resources or strategies from the KICKASS Happiness Toolkit will you explore to further enhance your happiness journey?

There you have it – your KICKASS guide to living life to the fullest, doing good, and finding your path to happiness. Embrace these principles, and watch as your life transforms into a beautiful, fulfilling adventure.

Chapter 9: Unleashing Your Inner Rebel

Section 1: The Maverick Mindset: How to think outside the box and challenge conventional wisdom.

Welcome to the KICKASS world of the Maverick Mindset. This is where we throw out the rulebook, and dive head-first into the realm of the unorthodox. It's time to give the finger to the status quo and embrace your inner rebel. Are you ready for it?

"The only way to deal with an unfree world is to become so absolutely free that your very existence is an act of rebellion." - Albert Camus

To become a true maverick, you need to understand what the Maverick Mindset is all about. It's a KICKASS approach to life that defies societal norms and challenges conventional wisdom. It's about being fearless, taking risks, and daring to be different. It's about breaking free from the shackles of conformity and daring to explore the uncharted territory. It's about embracing the unknown and venturing into the abyss with nothing but your wits, courage, and determination.

Here are some KICKASS tips to help you develop the Maverick Mindset:

a. Question everything: Don't just accept things at face value. Be curious, and question the status quo. Why does this work this way? Can it be done differently? What if we tried this instead? These questions will push you to explore alternative solutions and develop innovative ideas.

b. Embrace failure: Mavericks aren't afraid to fail. They understand that failure is just a stepping stone to success. So don't shy away from taking risks, even if it means you might fail. Remember, "I didn't fail. I just found 10,000 ways that won't work." - Thomas Edison

c. Be fearless: Mavericks don't back down from challenges. They don't let fear hold them back. Embrace the fear, and use it as fuel to drive you forward. As the legendary Bruce Lee once said, "Do not pray for an easy life, pray for the strength to endure a difficult one."

d. Stay true to yourself: Mavericks don't compromise their values or beliefs to fit in. They stay true to themselves, no matter what. Don't be afraid to stand up for what you believe in and to express your unique point of view.

Now that you have a better understanding of the Maverick Mindset, it's time to put it into action. Here are some KICKASS exercises to help you unleash your inner rebel:

1. The Maverick List: Write down 10 things you've always wanted to do but were too afraid or hesitant to try. This could be anything from skydiving to starting your own business. Then, make it your mission to cross off at least one item from the list each month.

2. The 180-Degree Challenge: Identify a conventional belief or practice that you disagree with. Then, do the exact opposite for a week. This will force you to think creatively and challenge the status quo.

3. The Discomfort Zone: Each day for a week, put yourself in a situation that makes you feel uncomfortable. This could be anything from striking up a conversation with a stranger to wearing an unconventional outfit. Embrace the discomfort and learn to thrive in it.

By incorporating these KICKASS exercises into your life, you'll be well on your way to developing a Maverick Mindset. Remember, it's not about following the herd; it's about forging your own path and embracing your unique talents.

"Here's to the crazy ones, the misfits, the rebels, the troublemakers, the round pegs in the square holes... the ones who see things differently — they're not fond of rules... You can quote them, disagree with them, glorify or vilify them, but the only thing you can't do is ignore them because they change things... they push the human race forward, and while some may see them as the crazy ones, we see genius, because the ones who are crazy enough to think that they can change the world, are the ones who do." — Steve Jobs

Now, let's move on to the next section of this KICKASS chapter: Breaking the Rules.

Section 2: Breaking the Rules: Knowing when to defy societal norms and forge your own path.

Alright, you badass rule-breaker! It's time to delve deeper into the art of defying societal norms and forging your own path. Breaking the rules doesn't mean being reckless or irresponsible; it's about knowing when to challenge the status quo and step outside the boundaries that limit your growth and potential.

"Learn the rules like a pro, so you can break them like an artist." - Pablo Picasso

To help you master the art of breaking the rules, here are some KICKASS principles to live by:

a. Know which rules to break: Not all rules are meant to be broken. It's crucial to understand which rules are holding you back and which ones serve a purpose. Be strategic in your rule-breaking and focus on the ones that stifle your creativity, individuality, and growth.

b. Trust your instincts: Your gut feeling can be a powerful compass in the rule-breaking journey. If something feels wrong or limiting, trust your instincts and challenge the norm. Sometimes, your intuition knows best.

c. Embrace the consequences: Breaking the rules might come with consequences, but that's part of the game. Accept the potential backlash and be prepared to stand your ground. As the iconic Mae West said, "When I'm good, I'm very good, but when I'm bad, I'm better."

d. Surround yourself with fellow rule-breakers: Find like-minded individuals who share your rebellious spirit. They will not only support and encourage your rule-breaking endeavors but also challenge and inspire you with their own daring feats.

Now that we've covered the principles of breaking the rules, let's dive into some KICKASS exercises to help you put these concepts into action:

1. The Rule-Breaking Journal: Keep a journal where you document the rules you've broken, the reasons behind it, and the outcomes (positive or negative). Reflect on your experiences and identify patterns or lessons you can learn from them.

2. The Rule-Breaking Audit: Take a look at your daily routine and identify any rules or norms that you blindly follow. Are they serving you well, or are they limiting your growth and happiness? Challenge these norms and experiment with breaking them to see how it impacts your life.

3. The Rebel Role Model: Identify a person, either someone you know personally or a famous figure, who embodies the rule-breaking spirit you admire. Study their life, their mindset, and their actions. What can you learn from them and apply in your own life?

By embracing these KICKASS principles and exercises, you'll be well on your way to mastering the art of breaking the rules and forging your own path. Remember, as the legendary Frank Sinatra sang, "I did it my way."

Now, let's continue our KICKASS journey and dive into the next section: Creativity Unleashed.

Section 3: Creativity Unleashed: Unlocking your unique talents and embracing your inner artist.

Get ready to unleash your inner artist and set your creativity free! This KICKASS section is all about tapping into your unique talents and discovering new ways to express yourself. Remember, creativity isn't just about art, music, or writing – it's about finding innovative solutions, thinking outside the box, and turning the ordinary into the extraordinary.

"Creativity is allowing yourself to make mistakes. Art is knowing which ones to keep." - Scott Adams

To help you unleash your creativity, here are some KICKASS tips to get those creative juices flowing:

a. Break free from your comfort zone: To unlock your creative potential, you need to step outside your comfort zone and explore new experiences, ideas, and perspectives. Try new things, challenge yourself, and never be afraid to take risks.

b. Surround yourself with inspiration: Fill your environment with things that inspire and ignite your creativity. This could be anything from artwork to books, music, or even the company of creative individuals. The more inspired you are, the more likely you are to tap into your creative genius.

c. Make time for creativity: Schedule regular "creative sessions" in your daily routine, where you dedicate time to exploring, experimenting, and expressing yourself. This could be as simple as a 15-minute doodling session or an hour-long writing spree.

d. Embrace imperfection: Don't get caught up in the pursuit of perfection. Embrace the messy, imperfect nature of creativity, and understand that it's a process of trial and error. As the renowned author Neil Gaiman said, "Make glorious, amazing mistakes. Make mistakes nobody's ever made before."

Now that you've got the KICKASS tips, let's dive into some exercises to help you unleash your creativity:

1. The Creative Playground: Choose a creative activity that you've never tried before, such as painting, dancing, or writing poetry. Set aside time to explore and play with this new form of expression, without any pressure or expectation.

2. The Creative Mashup: Combine two or more unrelated ideas, concepts, or objects, and try to create something new and unique. This could be a fusion of different art styles, a blend of genres in music, or even a mix of unusual ingredients in a recipe.

3. The Creative Constraints: Pick a creative task and impose some constraints on yourself, such as using only a limited color palette, writing a story in 100 words, or creating a piece of art using only found objects. Constraints can often ignite creativity by forcing you to think outside the box.

By following these KICKASS tips and exercises, you'll be well on your way to unlocking your unique talents and embracing your inner artist. Remember, creativity is a journey of exploration and self-expression — so enjoy the ride!

Now, let's move on to the final section of this KICKASS chapter: Innovate or Die.

Section 4: Innovate or Die: How to stay ahead of the curve and constantly reinvent yourself.

Welcome to the KICKASS world of innovation, where you either ride the wave of change or get crushed by it. Now, you might be thinking, "Mickey, why so dramatic?" Well, my friend, the truth is simple: in today's fast-paced world, if you're not moving forward, you're falling behind. So buckle up, buttercup, because we're about to dive headfirst into the exhilarating, no-holds-barred journey of self-reinvention and staying ahead of the curve.

First things first, let's get one thing straight: reinventing yourself doesn't mean you're throwing away everything you've ever known or accomplished. Far from it. It's about taking what you've learned and experienced, and using it as a foundation to build something even more KICKASS.

Now, I don't know about you, but I don't want to live a life where I'm constantly playing catch-up. I want to be the one setting the pace, and you should too. So let's get down to it. Here are some KICKASS strategies to help you stay ahead of the curve and constantly reinvent yourself:

1. Embrace change like a long-lost friend Remember that change is inevitable, and it's the only constant in life.

Don't resist it; welcome it with open arms. In fact, go out and seek it. The more you expose yourself to new experiences and ideas, the more adaptable and innovative you become. So try new things, step out of your comfort zone, and shake things up. After all, the only way to discover your true potential is to test your limits.

2. Stay hungry for knowledge Never stop learning. I can't emphasize this enough. In today's rapidly changing world, knowledge is power. Make a habit of devouring books, attending workshops, and surrounding yourself with people who challenge and inspire you. Keep an open mind and be willing to learn from anyone and everyone. And don't forget to apply what you've learned to your own life. As the great Bruce Lee once said, "Absorb what is useful, discard what is not, and add what is uniquely your own."

3. Cultivate a growth mindset Having a fixed mindset is the kiss of death when it comes to staying ahead of the curve. Don't fall into the trap of thinking that your abilities and intelligence are set in stone. Embrace the idea that you can always improve and grow. Failure isn't a sign that you're not good enough; it's an opportunity to learn and become better. So don't be afraid to make mistakes, take risks, and push the envelope. Remember, fortune favors the bold.

4. Make self-reflection a daily practice Set aside time each day to reflect on your thoughts, feelings, and actions. This will help you gain valuable insights into your strengths, weaknesses, and areas for improvement. Be brutally honest with yourself about where you're falling short and what you need to do to level up. Self-reflection is the key to self-awareness, and self-awareness is the key to growth and reinvention.

5. Surround yourself with forward-thinking, ambitious people You've probably heard the saying, "You're the average of the five people you spend the most time with." Well, it's true. If you want to stay ahead of the curve, you need to surround yourself with people who share your drive and ambition. These are the people who will challenge you, inspire you, and push you to achieve your full potential. So ditch the naysayers and energy vampires, and start building your KICKASS dream team.

Now that you have a roadmap for staying ahead of the curve and reinventing yourself, it's time to put these KICKASS strategies into action. Remember, there's no time like the present to start making moves and shaping your future. Here are a few more tips to help you on your journey:

6. Develop your personal brand In the digital age, your personal brand is everything. It's how you present yourself to the world and how others perceive you. So invest time in cultivating a strong, authentic personal

brand that reflects your values, passions, and unique strengths. Use social media, networking, and personal projects to showcase your expertise and build a reputation as a thought leader in your field.

7. Stay on top of trends and emerging technologies Don't get left behind in the dust of obsolescence. Keep your finger on the pulse of the latest trends and technologies in your industry and beyond. Subscribe to relevant blogs, podcasts, and newsletters, and attend conferences and networking events to stay informed and connected. By staying ahead of the game, you'll position yourself as a forward-thinking leader and increase your chances of long-term success.

8. Keep an idea journal Great ideas often come at the most unexpected times. Keep a journal or note-taking app handy to jot down your thoughts and ideas as they arise. Review your notes regularly and look for patterns and connections that could lead to innovative solutions or fresh perspectives. You never know when inspiration will strike, so be prepared to capture it when it does.

9. Take calculated risks Innovation and risk-taking go hand in hand. You can't expect to break new ground without taking some chances along the way. That said, it's essential to weigh the potential rewards against the risks before making a move. Be bold, but also be smart. Learn to trust your instincts and embrace the uncertainty that comes with pushing boundaries.

10. Never stop pushing your limits If you want to stay ahead of the curve, you can't afford to rest on your laurels. Continuously challenge yourself to learn new skills, tackle ambitious projects, and explore unfamiliar territory. Set high, yet achievable goals and work tirelessly to reach them. Remember, the only limits that truly exist are the ones you impose on yourself.

There you have it, folks — a KICKASS guide to staying ahead of the curve and constantly reinventing yourself. Now, it's up to you to take these strategies and make them your own. So go forth, my fellow rebels, and show the world what you're made of. And always remember, in the immortal words of the legendary Steve Jobs, "Stay hungry, stay foolish."

Bonus Content: The KICKASS Recipe for Unleashing Your Inner Maverick

Looking for that extra edge to supercharge your journey of reinvention? Look no further. Here's a KICKASS bonus recipe to help you unleash your inner maverick and take your game to a whole new level:

Ingredients:

1. A generous helping of courage
2. A dash of curiosity
3. A pinch of adaptability
4. A sprinkle of resilience

5. A heaping spoonful of creativity
6. A touch of resourcefulness

Instructions:

1. Mix all the ingredients in a large bowl of self-belief.
2. Stir in a healthy dose of optimism.
3. Add a splash of gratitude for good measure.
4. Bake in the oven of hard work, perseverance, and discipline.
5. Serve hot, garnished with a zest for life and a never-ending appetite for success.

Chapter 9 Summary:

In Chapter 9, we dove headfirst into the world of innovation and self-reinvention. We explored the importance of cultivating a maverick mindset, breaking the rules when necessary, unleashing your creativity, and staying ahead of the curve in a rapidly changing world. Through a series of KICKASS strategies, we learned how to embrace change, stay hungry for knowledge, cultivate a growth mindset, practice self-reflection, surround ourselves with ambitious people, develop a personal brand, stay on top of trends, maintain an idea journal, take calculated risks, and continuously push our limits.

Five KICKASS Questions to Reflect on:

1. What is one area of your life where you could benefit from embracing change and thinking outside the box? How will you approach this challenge?

2. How can you cultivate a growth mindset and use failure as a learning opportunity instead of a setback?

3. What steps will you take to surround yourself with forward-thinking, ambitious people who will push you to reach your full potential?

4. How can you leverage your unique talents and strengths to create a personal brand that sets you apart from the competition?

5. What is one bold, calculated risk you're willing to take to stay ahead of the curve and reinvent yourself?

Take some time to reflect on these questions, and remember that staying ahead of the curve is an ongoing process. Keep pushing yourself to learn, grow, and embrace the unpredictable journey of self-reinvention. Stay KICKASS, my friends.

Chapter 10: The Power of Vulnerability

Section 1: The Strength in Softness: Embracing vulnerability as a source of courage and connection.

Welcome, my KICKASS friends, to this pivotal chapter in our kickass journey! It's time to dive into the most liberating and empowering experience of your life — embracing vulnerability. Yeah, you read that right. Vulnerability. Let's strip off our emotional armor, expose our true selves, and reap the benefits of living a life full of courage, connection, and authenticity. Buckle up, because this is going to be one hell of a ride.

In a world that glorifies toughness and resilience, vulnerability often gets a bad rap. We're taught to hide our weaknesses, to act like we have our shit together all the time. But guess what? That's just an illusion. No one, and I mean NO ONE, is immune to struggles, setbacks, or heartaches. It's time to stop pretending and start living with our hearts wide open.

Vulnerability is the essence of being human. When we embrace our vulnerability, we tap into a source of power that allows us to connect more deeply with others, feel more alive, and ultimately achieve greater success and happiness. So let's dive into the wonderful world of vulnerability and discover the strength in softness.

"Vulnerability is not winning or losing; it's having the courage to show up and be seen when we have no control over the outcome." — Brené Brown

To help you embrace your vulnerability, here's a KICKASS exercise to get you started:

1. Find a quiet and comfortable space where you can sit and reflect.

2. Close your eyes and take a few deep breaths.

3. Think about a time when you felt vulnerable. It could be a moment of failure, rejection, or heartbreak.

4. Now, ask yourself: How did that moment of vulnerability make you feel? Did it make you feel small, weak, or embarrassed? Or did it push you to grow, learn, and become a better person?

5. Reflect on how embracing your vulnerability in that moment could have led to a deeper connection with others or even yourself.

6. Open your eyes and write down your thoughts and insights.

Repeat this exercise whenever you need a reminder of the KICKASS power of vulnerability. Remember, vulnerability is not a weakness – it's a source of strength, courage, and connection.

Now that we've laid the foundation for understanding the strength in softness, let's explore how ditching our emotional armor can lead to deeper connections in the next section. Stay tuned, and stay vulnerable, my friends!

Section 2: Ditching the Armor: Letting go of emotional barriers and opening up to deeper connections.

Alright, you KICKASS warriors, it's time to ditch that emotional armor that's been weighing you down for way too long. Let's face it – we all have our emotional barriers, those walls we put up to protect ourselves from getting hurt. But what if I told you that tearing down those walls can lead to deeper, more meaningful connections with others and a more fulfilling life?

You might be thinking, "But Mickey, that's some scary shit!" And you're damn right it is! But the rewards are worth it. Trust me.

So let's talk about how to let go of those emotional barriers and open up to deeper connections. Remember, this is a KICKASS journey, and we're in it together.

First and foremost, recognize that emotional armor is often rooted in fear. Fear of rejection, fear of being judged, fear of getting hurt. But as the old saying goes, "The only thing we have to fear is fear itself." So let's kick fear in the ass and embrace the unknown.

Here's a KICKASS exercise to help you ditch your emotional armor:

1. Grab a piece of paper and a pen or pencil.
2. Write down three emotional barriers you've built to protect yourself. It could be anything – avoiding deep

conversations, keeping people at arm's length, or hiding your true feelings.

3. Now, for each barrier, write down one action you can take to break it down. Be specific and be brave.

4. Commit to taking those actions and watch how your connections with others deepen and grow.

"Don't be afraid to let your guard down and show your vulnerability. It's the only way to let love in and truly connect with others." – Unknown

As you work on ditching your emotional armor, remember that it's okay to feel scared or uncertain. Embrace those feelings, and let them fuel your journey towards more authentic connections. And if you stumble along the way, don't beat yourself up. We're all human, and we're all learning.

So, my KICKASS friends, let's continue to break down those walls and open ourselves up to the world. With every barrier we tear down, we'll discover more about ourselves and forge deeper connections with others. Stay tuned for the next section, where we'll explore the incredible benefits of authenticity and vulnerability.

Section 3: The Authenticity Advantage: How being genuine and vulnerable can lead to greater success and happiness.

KICKASS people, you've made it this far – embracing vulnerability and ditching the emotional armor. Now, let's talk about the incredible rewards that come with being genuine and vulnerable: greater success and happiness. That's right, living authentically isn't just about feeling good — it's also about kicking ass in every aspect of your life.

When we embrace our true selves and let our vulnerability shine, we unlock a world of possibilities. People are drawn to authenticity, and they can sense when someone is genuine. By being open, honest, and vulnerable, we create meaningful connections, which can lead to incredible opportunities both personally and professionally.

So, let's dive into the advantages of authenticity and vulnerability, and discover how to reap the rewards of living a KICKASS life.

1. Trust: When we're genuine and vulnerable, people are more likely to trust us. Trust is the foundation of any successful relationship, whether it's with friends, family, or colleagues. By being authentic, you're showing others that you're willing to be honest and open, which strengthens the bond of trust.

2. Self-awareness: Embracing vulnerability allows us to see ourselves more clearly. We become more aware of our strengths and weaknesses, our passions and fears, our dreams and desires. This self-awareness is crucial for personal growth and success.

3. Resilience: By facing our fears and embracing vulnerability, we build resilience. When we're not afraid of failure, rejection, or criticism, we're more likely to

bounce back from setbacks and keep moving forward on our KICKASS journey.

4. Attraction: Authenticity is magnetic. People are drawn to those who are genuine, honest, and vulnerable. By being true to yourself, you'll attract like-minded individuals who share your values and passions, leading to deeper connections and greater opportunities.

Now, let's put this all into action with a KICKASS exercise:

1. Make a list of three areas in your life where you can be more authentic and vulnerable. It could be at work, in your relationships, or even with yourself.

2. For each area, identify one specific action you can take to embrace your authenticity and vulnerability.

3. Commit to taking those actions and notice the positive impact on your success and happiness.

"Authenticity is a collection of choices that we have to make every day. It's about the choice to show up and be real. The choice to be honest. The choice to let our true selves be seen."
– Brené Brown

My KICKASS friends, as we continue on this journey, remember that authenticity and vulnerability are the keys to unlocking a life of success and happiness. Keep practicing, keep pushing, and keep being your true, amazing self. Stay tuned for the next section, where we'll explore healing through vulnerability.

Section 4: Healing Through Vulnerability: Using openness and self-expression as a path to healing and growth.

Welcome back, my KICKASS warriors! We've embraced vulnerability, ditched our emotional armor, and discovered the authenticity advantage. Now, let's talk about one of the most powerful and transformative aspects of vulnerability: healing and growth.

Life is full of challenges, setbacks, and heartbreaks. It's inevitable. But the way we handle those experiences can make all the difference. When we allow ourselves to be vulnerable, we open the door to healing and growth. By facing our pain, fears, and insecurities, we can heal emotional wounds and become stronger, wiser, and more resilient.

So, let's explore how to use vulnerability as a path to healing and growth, and become the KICKASS individuals we're meant to be.

1. Acknowledge your pain: The first step to healing is admitting that you're hurting. It's okay to feel sad, angry, or scared. Give yourself permission to feel those emotions without judgment or shame.

2. Share your story: Open up to someone you trust – a friend, family member, or therapist – and share your feelings and experiences. This act of vulnerability can be incredibly healing and cathartic, as it helps to release pent-up emotions and create a sense of connection.

3. Practice self-compassion: Be kind to yourself. Recognize that you're human, and it's normal to struggle and feel pain. Treat yourself with the same compassion and understanding you would offer to a friend in need.

4. Embrace the lessons: Every challenge, setback, and heartbreak contains valuable lessons. By embracing vulnerability, we can learn from these experiences and use them as stepping stones to growth and self-improvement.

Ready for a KICKASS exercise to help you heal through vulnerability?

1. Find a quiet, comfortable space where you can sit and reflect.

2. Close your eyes and take a few deep breaths.

3. Think about a painful or difficult experience from your past.

4. Ask yourself: What lessons can I learn from this experience? How can I use this pain to grow and become a stronger, more resilient person?

5. Write down your insights and reflections in a journal or notebook.

"Owning our story can be hard but not nearly as difficult as spending our lives running from it. Embracing our vulnerabilities is risky but not nearly as dangerous as giving up on love and belonging and joy — the experiences that make us the most vulnerable." — Brené Brown

Remember, my KICKASS friends, vulnerability is not only a source of courage and connection but also a powerful tool for healing and growth. As we continue on this journey, let's embrace our vulnerability, learn from our experiences, and become the best versions of ourselves. Keep on being KICKASS, and keep on growing.

KICKASS Bonus Content: The Vulnerability Challenge

Alright, my KICKASS friends, it's time for a little bonus content to help you truly embrace the power of vulnerability. I present to you: The Vulnerability Challenge!

For the next 30 days, I challenge you to do one thing every day that makes you feel vulnerable. It could be something as simple as having a deep conversation with a friend, admitting when you're wrong, or trying something new that scares you. The goal is to push your boundaries, face your fears, and become more comfortable with vulnerability.

To help you stay on track, here's a KICKASS Vulnerability Challenge Tracker:

1. Print out a calendar for the next 30 days.
2. Each day, write down the vulnerable action you took.
3. At the end of the 30 days, reflect on your growth, the connections you've made, and the lessons you've learned.

Now, let's wrap up Chapter 10 with a KICKASS summary and some thought-provoking questions:

Summary of Chapter 10: The Power of Vulnerability

1. The Strength in Softness: Embracing vulnerability as a source of courage and connection.

2. Ditching the Armor: Letting go of emotional barriers and opening up to deeper connections.

3. The Authenticity Advantage: How being genuine and vulnerable can lead to greater success and happiness.

4. Healing Through Vulnerability: Using openness and self-expression as a path to healing and growth.

Five KICKASS Questions to Reflect on:

1. In what areas of your life do you struggle with vulnerability? How can you work on embracing vulnerability in those areas?

2. What emotional barriers are holding you back from forming deeper connections with others? How can you start to break down those barriers?

3. How has being authentic and vulnerable helped you in your personal or professional life? Can you think of a specific example?

4. Reflect on a time when you used vulnerability as a path to healing and growth. What did you learn from that experience?

5. How can you continue to incorporate vulnerability into your daily life to foster greater courage, connection, and growth?

Keep reflecting on these questions, and don't forget to take the 30-day Vulnerability Challenge. Stay KICKASS, my friends, and embrace the power of vulnerability!

Chapter 11: Mastering Mindfulness

Section 1: The Zen Zone: An introduction to mindfulness and its benefits for well-being and happiness.

Welcome to the KICKASS world of mindfulness, my friend! It's time to buckle up and get ready for a wild ride that'll take you straight into the Zen Zone. This is where we'll dive deep into mindfulness and uncover all the amazing benefits it has to offer for your well-being and happiness. But first, let's get this party started with a badass quote that'll set the tone for the rest of this KICKASS chapter:

"In the midst of chaos, there is also opportunity." - Sun Tzu

Now that we're all fired up, let's dive right into the heart of the matter. What the hell is mindfulness, anyway? Well, it's a state of being that involves being fully present, aware of where we are, what we're doing, and not being overly reactive or overwhelmed by the situations that life throws at us. It's all about living in the moment, embracing the "now," and finding peace in the everyday hustle and bustle of life.

But why should you give a damn about mindfulness? Well, let me tell you, the benefits of mindfulness are KICKASS, to say the least. Here are some ways that mindfulness can help you kick some serious ass in life:

- Reduces stress and anxiety: When you're mindful, you're better equipped to deal with the curveballs life throws at you. You become a stress-busting machine, able to shrug off anxiety and keep your cool when the going gets tough.

- Improves focus and concentration: A mindful mind is a focused mind. By practicing mindfulness, you'll sharpen your mental skills, making it easier to concentrate on the task at hand and get shit done.

- Boosts emotional intelligence: By being more in tune with your emotions and those of others, you'll become a master of empathy and understanding. You'll forge deeper connections with those around you, making your relationships more meaningful and fulfilling.

- Enhances self-awareness: Mindfulness helps you get to know yourself better. You'll gain a deeper understanding of your thoughts, emotions, and behaviors, allowing you to make better decisions and live a more authentic, fulfilling life.

- Increases overall well-being and happiness: By being more present and engaged in life, you'll experience more joy, satisfaction, and fulfillment. You'll be able to truly savor each moment, making the most of your time on this crazy, beautiful planet.

Now that you've got a taste of what mindfulness can do for you, let's jump into some practical techniques that'll help you become a Zen master in no time!

Section 2: Mindfulness in Motion: Practical techniques for incorporating mindfulness into everyday life.

Alright, folks, now that you're pumped and ready to embrace the KICKASS world of mindfulness, let's talk about some practical techniques that'll help you incorporate mindfulness into your everyday life. Remember, it's all about taking action and putting these badass strategies to work. So, without further ado, let's dive in!

a. The KICKASS One-Minute Breathing Exercise: Sometimes, all it takes is a minute to change your entire perspective. Whenever you feel overwhelmed, stressed, or disconnected, take a minute to focus on your breath. Breathe in deeply through your nose, filling your lungs with fresh air, then exhale slowly through your mouth, releasing any tension or negative energy. Repeat this for a full minute, and you'll be amazed at how quickly your mind clears and your body relaxes.

b. The Mindful Eating Challenge: We all gotta eat, right? So why not turn mealtime into an opportunity to practice mindfulness? Next time you sit down for a meal, take a moment to truly appreciate the food in front of you. Consider its colors, textures, and flavors. Chew slowly, savoring each bite, and be fully present with the experience. You'll not only enjoy your meal more, but you'll also become more in tune with your body's hunger and fullness cues.

c. The Mindful Commute: Turn your daily commute into a mindfulness exercise by focusing on the sensations around you. Notice the sounds, smells, and sights that you encounter, and fully immerse yourself in the experience. If you're driving, feel the vibrations of the car beneath you and the pressure of your foot on the pedal. If you're walking or biking, feel the wind on your face and the rhythm of your footsteps or pedaling. Embrace each moment as an opportunity to practice mindfulness in motion.

d. The Body Scan: Here's another KICKASS technique that you can practice pretty much anywhere. Take a few minutes to do a mental body scan, starting at the top of your head and working your way down to your toes. Focus on each body part and release any tension you might be holding there. This exercise is not only a great way to practice mindfulness, but it's also an excellent method for releasing stress and tension throughout your body.

e. The Five Senses Check-In: Several times a day, take a moment to check in with your five senses. What do you see, hear, smell, taste, and feel? Engaging with your senses is a powerful way to ground yourself in the present moment and snap out of autopilot mode.

Alright, my KICKASS friend, now you've got a bunch of practical techniques for incorporating mindfulness into your everyday life. Give them a try, and you'll be well on your way to mastering mindfulness and reaping all its incredible benefits.

Section 3: The Power of Now: How to be fully present and engaged in each moment.

Welcome to the next level of KICKASS mindfulness, my friend! In this section, we'll talk about the Power of Now and how you can harness it to become fully present and engaged in each and every moment of your life. It's time to take control, live in the present, and make every second count. Let's kick this section off with another badass quote to get us in the right mindset:

"Realize deeply that the present moment is all you have. Make the NOW the primary focus of your life." - Eckhart Tolle

Now that we're all fired up, let's dive into some strategies for tapping into the Power of Now and living a fully present, engaged life:

a. Cultivate a Non-Judgmental Awareness: To truly embrace the present moment, we need to let go of our judgments and simply observe our experiences as they are. This means not labeling our thoughts, emotions, or sensations as good or bad, but instead, accepting them without judgment. Practice this non-judgmental awareness in your daily life, and you'll find it easier to stay present and engaged in each moment.

b. Embrace Impermanence: Life is constantly changing, and nothing lasts forever. By recognizing and accepting the impermanent nature of our experiences, we can let go of our attachment to the past and future and fully embrace the present moment. Remember, the only constant in life is change, so make the most of the now while it lasts.

c. Cultivate Gratitude: Practicing gratitude is a powerful way to ground yourself in the present moment. Take time each day to reflect on the things you're grateful for, big or small. This simple act can help you shift your focus from what you lack to what you already have, making it easier to stay present and engaged in the now.

d. Mindful Listening: Make a conscious effort to truly listen when someone is speaking to you. Rather than thinking about what you're going to say next or getting lost in your own thoughts, focus on the other person's words, tone, and body language. This not only helps you stay present in the moment but also deepens your connection with others.

e. Set Intentions: Begin each day with a clear intention to be fully present and engaged in every moment. By setting this intention, you'll be more likely to notice when your mind starts to wander and gently bring it back to the present moment.

Alright, you KICKASS mindfulness warrior! Now you've got the tools and strategies to harness the Power of Now and live a fully present, engaged life. It's time to say goodbye to living in the past or worrying about the future – the present moment is where the magic happens.

Section 4: Mindful Relationships: Cultivating deeper connections and empathy through mindfulness.

You've made it this far, my KICKASS friend, and now it's time to bring it all together by applying mindfulness to the most important aspect of our lives – our relationships. Get ready to learn how to cultivate deeper connections and empathy through mindfulness, making your relationships more rewarding and fulfilling than ever before. Let's kick off this final section with an inspiring quote:

"Attention is the rarest and purest form of generosity." - Simone Weil

Now that we're all pumped up, let's dive into some KICKASS strategies for fostering mindful relationships:

a. Active Listening: We've already touched on mindful listening in the previous section, but it's worth repeating – truly listening to others is a powerful way to cultivate deeper connections. When you actively listen, you give your full attention to the other person, making them feel valued, heard, and understood. This simple act can work wonders in strengthening your relationships.

b. Nonviolent Communication: Practice expressing your thoughts and feelings in a non-threatening, non-judgmental way. By using "I" statements and focusing on your own emotions rather than blaming or criticizing others, you'll encourage open and honest communication, fostering empathy and understanding in your relationships.

c. Be Fully Present: Give your undivided attention to the person you're with, whether it's your partner, friend, or family member. Put away your phone, forget about your to-do list, and be fully present with them. By being truly present in your interactions, you'll create deeper connections and make others feel valued and appreciated.

d. Practice Empathy: Put yourself in the other person's shoes and try to understand their thoughts, feelings, and perspectives. By practicing empathy, you'll develop a deeper understanding of those around you, strengthening your connections and fostering a sense of compassion and support.

e. Embrace Vulnerability: Be open and honest about your own thoughts, feelings, and experiences, even when it's scary or uncomfortable. Sharing your vulnerability can help build trust, deepen connections, and create a safe space for open communication in your relationships.

f. Cultivate Loving-Kindness: Make a conscious effort to cultivate loving-kindness and compassion towards yourself and others. By practicing loving-kindness meditation or simply setting an intention to approach your relationships with love and compassion, you'll create a positive, nurturing environment where connections can flourish.

Congratulations, my KICKASS friend! You've now mastered the art of mindfulness and have all the tools you need to create a life filled with well-being, happiness, and deeper connections. Remember, the key to success is putting these strategies into action and making mindfulness a part of your daily life. So go out there and live your best, most mindful life — you've got this!

And remember, as the legendary Bruce Lee once said: "To hell with circumstances; I create opportunities." So seize the opportunities mindfulness presents, and watch your life transform in KICKASS ways.

BONUS CONTENT: Kickass Mindfulness Hacks

Alright, my KICKASS friend, you've made it through Chapter 11, and as a reward, I'm throwing in some bonus content to take your mindfulness game to the next level. Here are a few additional hacks to supercharge your mindfulness practice:

1. Set Mindfulness Reminders: Set alarms or reminders on your phone to practice mindfulness throughout the day. You can use these reminders to take a deep breath, do a body scan, or simply refocus on the present moment.

2. Create a Mindful Morning Routine: Start your day off on the right foot by incorporating mindfulness into your morning routine. This could include meditation, mindful stretching, or simply enjoying a cup of coffee or tea with full awareness.

3. Join a Mindfulness Community: Connect with others who share your interest in mindfulness by joining a local meditation group, attending workshops, or participating in online forums. Sharing your experiences and learning from others can help keep you motivated and inspired on your mindfulness journey.

4. Read Mindfulness Books: Expand your knowledge and deepen your practice by reading books on mindfulness and meditation. From ancient texts to contemporary bestsellers, there's a wealth of wisdom waiting for you to explore.

5. Keep a Mindfulness Journal: Record your thoughts, feelings, and insights as you embark on your mindfulness journey. Journaling can help you track your progress, identify patterns, and gain deeper insights into your experiences.

Chapter 11 Summary:

In Chapter 11, we explored the KICKASS world of mindfulness, diving into its benefits, practical techniques, and strategies for living a fully present, engaged life. We discussed how mindfulness can improve your well-being, happiness, and relationships, and provided you with a toolbox of techniques to help you master mindfulness in your everyday life.

Five KICKASS Questions to Reflect on:

As a recap, here are five questions to help you reflect on the key takeaways from this chapter:

1. How can mindfulness benefit your well-being, happiness, and relationships?

2. What are some practical techniques for incorporating mindfulness into your everyday life?

3. How can embracing the Power of Now help you become fully present and engaged in each moment?

4. What are some strategies for cultivating deeper connections and empathy in your relationships through mindfulness?

5. How can the bonus content and mindfulness hacks enhance your mindfulness practice?

Keep these questions in mind as you continue your journey towards mindfulness mastery, and remember to live your life to the fullest by embracing the KICKASS Power of Now!

Chapter 12: The Art of Letting Go

Section 1: The Freedom of Forgiveness: Learning to forgive yourself and others for a happier, healthier life.

Listen up, because I'm about to tell you something that's going to change your life: Forgiveness is the ultimate KICKASS power move. Yeah, you heard me right. Letting go of grudges, bitterness, and resentment isn't just a nice thing to do – it's a must if you want to live your best life. So, buckle up and get ready for a deep dive into the world of forgiveness. We're going to cover why it's so important, how to do it, and some KICKASS exercises to help you along the way.

Forgiveness is more than just saying "I'm sorry" or "I forgive you." It's a whole attitude shift. It means letting go of the past, moving on, and accepting that everyone makes mistakes – including you. It's about understanding that holding onto resentment and anger only hurts you, not the person who wronged you. In other words, forgiveness is the key to unlocking a happier, healthier life.

But why is forgiveness so KICKASS? Well, for starters, it's good for your physical health. Studies show that people who forgive are less likely to have high blood pressure, heart problems, and weakened immune systems. It's also great for your mental health. Forgiving yourself and others can lower stress levels, reduce anxiety, and improve your overall mood. Plus, it can improve your relationships and help you become a more compassionate person.

So, how do you start embracing forgiveness? It's not always easy, but these steps will get you on the right track:

1. Reflect on the situation: Think about what happened and how it made you feel. Remember that everyone makes mistakes, and it's important to be honest with yourself about your own role in the situation.

2. Express your feelings: Whether it's through journaling, talking to a trusted friend, or venting in a safe space, let out your emotions. This will help you process what happened and make it easier to move on.

3. Decide to forgive: Make a conscious decision to let go of your resentment and anger. This doesn't mean you're condoning the other person's actions, but you're choosing not to let them control your life anymore.

4. Practice empathy: Put yourself in the other person's shoes and try to understand their perspective. This can help you let go of your negative feelings and foster compassion.

5. Repeat as needed: Forgiveness isn't always a one-time thing. Sometimes you'll need to remind yourself of your decision and practice forgiveness over and over again.

Now, let's talk about some KICKASS exercises to help you forgive:

- The Forgiveness Letter: Write a letter to the person who hurt you, expressing your feelings and your decision to forgive them. You don't have to send it – the act of writing it is therapeutic enough.

- The Gratitude Journal: Focus on the positive by keeping a daily journal of things you're grateful for. This will help you cultivate a more forgiving and compassionate mindset.

- Meditation: Practice mindfulness meditation to help you let go of negative thoughts and emotions. There are plenty of guided meditations available online specifically designed for forgiveness.

Remember this quote from the legendary Nelson Mandela: "Resentment is like drinking poison and then hoping it will kill your enemies." Forgiveness isn't about the other person – it's about you, and your ability to live a KICKASS life. So, take the leap, embrace forgiveness, and watch as your life transforms for the better.

Section 2: The Minimalist Mentality: Embracing simplicity and decluttering your life for more peace and focus.

Alright, folks, get ready for some KICKASS truth: The key to a more peaceful and focused life isn't buying more stuff or juggling a million responsibilities – it's embracing simplicity and decluttering your life. That's right, we're diving into the Minimalist Mentality, and I promise you, it's going to be a game-changer.

Minimalism isn't about living in an empty, sterile environment or giving up everything you love. It's about cutting out the excess, focusing on what truly matters, and living a life full of purpose and intention. It's about recognizing that more stuff doesn't equal more happiness, and learning to be content with less.

So, how do you start embracing the Minimalist Mentality and decluttering your life? Here's a KICKASS step-by-step guide to help you on your journey:

1. Assess your priorities: Take a good, hard look at your life and figure out what truly matters to you. What do you value the most? What brings you the most joy? Focus on these things and let go of the rest.

2. Declutter your physical space: Go through your possessions and get rid of anything that doesn't serve a purpose or bring you joy. Be ruthless – if it's not adding value to your life, it's time to say goodbye.

3. Simplify your digital life: Clean up your email inbox, unfollow social media accounts that don't enrich your life, and delete unnecessary apps from your phone. Remember, minimalism is about quality over quantity.

4. Simplify your commitments: Take a look at your calendar and evaluate your commitments. Are there activities or obligations that are draining your time and energy without adding value to your life? It's time to let them go.

5. Set boundaries: Learn to say no and protect your time and energy. It's okay to prioritize your own well-being and peace of mind.

Now, let's dive into some KICKASS exercises to help you embrace the Minimalist Mentality:

- The 30-Day Minimalism Challenge: Each day for 30 days, get rid of one item from your home. This will help you build decluttering habits and become more intentional about what you keep in your space.

- The One-In, One Out Rule: Whenever you bring a new item into your home, get rid of something else. This will help you maintain a clutter-free environment and make more thoughtful purchasing decisions.

- Mindful Consumption: Before making a purchase, ask yourself if the item truly aligns with your values and brings you joy. This will help you make more intentional choices and avoid accumulating unnecessary possessions.

To quote the great Bruce Lee, "It's not the daily increase but the daily decrease. Hack away at the inessentials." Embracing the Minimalist Mentality is all about cutting away the excess and focusing on what truly matters. So, get ready to declutter, simplify, and live a more peaceful, focused, and KICKASS life.

Section 3: Letting Go of Control: How to trust the process and surrender to the flow of life.

Alright, my friends, it's time for another KICKASS revelation: One of the keys to a more fulfilling and peaceful life is learning to let go of control. You see, life is unpredictable, and no matter how much we try to micromanage every aspect of it, we can't control everything. So, buckle up and get ready to dive into the art of surrendering to the flow of life.

Letting go of control doesn't mean you stop caring or become passive. It's about recognizing that there are things beyond your control and learning to adapt, trust the process, and find peace in uncertainty. It's about being open to change, embracing spontaneity, and enjoying the journey instead of constantly worrying about the destination.

So, how do you start letting go of control and surrendering to the flow of life? Here's a KICKASS step-by-step guide to help you on your journey:

1. Practice mindfulness: Focus on the present moment and let go of worries about the past or the future. This will help you become more aware of your thoughts and feelings, and make it easier to release control.

2. Embrace imperfection: Accept that you're not perfect, and neither is anyone else. Recognize that it's okay to make mistakes, and that life is full of unexpected twists and turns.

3. Trust yourself: Believe in your ability to handle whatever comes your way. You're more resilient and adaptable than you give yourself credit for.

4. Cultivate gratitude: Focus on the positive aspects of your life and be grateful for what you have, rather than constantly striving for more.

5. Learn to adapt: When things don't go as planned, instead of resisting, find a way to make the best of the situation.

Now, let's explore some KICKASS exercises to help you let go of control:

- The Worry Box: Write down your worries on slips of paper and put them in a designated "worry box." This physical act of letting go of your concerns can help you release control and trust the process.

- Daily Meditation: Practice meditation to help you focus on the present moment and let go of the need to control everything. There are many guided meditations available online that can help you with this.

- The Serenity Prayer: Repeat this well-known prayer to yourself as a reminder to let go of control: "Grant me the serenity to accept the things I cannot change, courage to change the things I can, and wisdom to know the difference."

Remember this KICKASS quote from the Tao Te Ching: "Life is a series of natural and spontaneous changes. Don't resist them; that only creates sorrow. Let reality be reality. Let things flow naturally forward in whatever way they like." So, take a deep breath, let go of control, and watch as your life becomes more fulfilling and peaceful.

Section 4: The Serenity of Acceptance: Finding peace and happiness by accepting what you cannot change

You've made it to the final section of our KICKASS journey into the Art of Letting Go, and now it's time to talk about the Serenity of Acceptance. Get ready to unlock a new level of peace and happiness by learning how to accept what you cannot change.

Acceptance isn't about giving up or being passive. It's about recognizing that some things are beyond our control, and instead of wasting energy fighting against them, we can find peace by embracing them. It's about learning to dance in the rain, rather than cursing the storm.

So, how do you start cultivating the Serenity of Acceptance? Here's a KICKASS step-by-step guide to help you on your journey:

1. Acknowledge your feelings: When facing a challenging situation, allow yourself to feel the emotions that come with it. Don't suppress them – embrace them, and recognize that it's okay to feel what you're feeling.

2. Assess the situation: Determine what aspects of the situation are within your control and what parts are beyond your control. Focus your energy on the things you can change, and let go of the rest.

3. Practice self-compassion: Be kind to yourself and acknowledge that you're doing your best. Remember, you're only human, and it's okay to not have everything figured out.

4. Focus on the present: Don't dwell on the past or worry about the future. Instead, concentrate on what you can do right now to make the best of your current situation.

5. Embrace change: Recognize that life is full of change, and learn to find peace in the uncertainty. Remember, without change, there would be no growth.

Now, let's dive into some KICKASS exercises to help you cultivate the Serenity of Acceptance:

- The Acceptance Meditation: Find a quiet space and take a few deep breaths. Focus on your breath and repeat the mantra "I accept what I cannot change" as you exhale. This will help you let go of resistance and find peace in acceptance.

- The Three Good Things Exercise: Each day, write down three good things that happened to you. This will help shift your focus from what you cannot control to the positive aspects of your life.

- The Five-Minute Journal: Spend five minutes each day reflecting on your day, acknowledging your emotions, and expressing gratitude. This will help you cultivate acceptance and find peace in your daily life.

To quote the brilliant American theologian Reinhold Niebuhr, "God grant me the serenity to accept the things I cannot change, courage to change the things I can, and wisdom to know the difference." Embracing the Serenity of Acceptance is a KICKASS way to find peace and happiness in your life, no matter what challenges you face.

Congratulations! You've made it through the entire chapter on The Art of Letting Go. Now, take these KICKASS lessons to heart and start living a happier, more peaceful, and more fulfilling life. You've got this!

Bonus Content: Kickass Tips for Mastering the Art of Letting Go

Before we wrap up Chapter 12, here's some KICKASS bonus content to help you fully embrace the Art of Letting Go:

1. Practice daily mindfulness: Incorporate meditation, deep breathing, or journaling into your daily routine to help you stay present and let go of worries about the past or future.

2. Surround yourself with positive influences: Seek out people who encourage and support your journey towards letting go, and avoid those who bring negativity into your life.

3. Stay open to new experiences: Embrace spontaneity and be willing to step outside your comfort zone. This will help you release control and trust the flow of life.

4. Celebrate your progress: Recognize and reward yourself for the steps you've taken towards letting go. Every small victory counts!

5. Remain patient and persistent: The Art of Letting Go is a lifelong journey. Don't get discouraged if you don't see immediate results – keep at it, and remember that progress is often slow but steady.

Chapter 12 Summary: The Art of Letting Go

In this KICKASS chapter, we explored four key aspects of the Art of Letting Go:

1. The Freedom of Forgiveness: We learned how to forgive ourselves and others, paving the way for a happier, healthier life.

2. The Minimalist Mentality: We embraced simplicity and decluttered our lives for more peace and focus.

3. Letting Go of Control: We discovered how to trust the process and surrender to the flow of life.

4. The Serenity of Acceptance: We found peace and happiness by accepting what we cannot change.

Five KICKASS Questions to Reflect on:

Now, let's test your KICKASS knowledge with these five questions:

1. What is the first step to embracing the Freedom of Forgiveness?

2. How can the 30-Day Minimalism Challenge help you adopt the Minimalist Mentality?

3. What is one exercise that can help you let go of control and trust the process?

4. What is the main goal of practicing the Serenity of Acceptance?

5. Name one of the Kickass Tips for Mastering the Art of Letting Go.

Congratulations on completing Chapter 12, my friends! You're now equipped with the KICKASS knowledge and tools to embrace the Art of Letting Go and live a more peaceful, fulfilling, and happy life. Keep up the fantastic work!

Chapter 13: Building Bulletproof Confidence

Section 1: Unshakable Self-Belief: Developing a rock-solid foundation of self-confidence.

KICKASS! That's right, get ready to dive headfirst into this KICKASS chapter on building bulletproof confidence. We're starting off with a bang, focusing on developing an unshakable self-belief that will serve as the rock-solid foundation for your self-confidence. So buckle up, because you're in for a wild ride!

You might be wondering, "What exactly is unshakable self-belief?" Well, my friend, unshakable self-belief is the unwavering conviction that you are capable of achieving anything you set your mind to. It's the unbreakable trust in your own abilities and the refusal to let fear or doubt hold you back. Remember the immortal words of Henry Ford: "Whether you think you can, or you think you can't—you're right." Your self-belief will shape your reality, so let's make it KICKASS!

To start building that unshakable self-belief, follow these KICKASS steps:

A. Rewrite Your Internal Dialogue: You know that little voice in your head that tells you you're not good enough, smart enough, or strong enough? Tell it to f*ck off! Replace that negative self-talk with empowering affirmations that reinforce your self-belief. Every time you catch yourself thinking negatively, stop and replace it with a KICKASS, positive thought.

B. Set KICKASS Goals: Set ambitious but achievable goals that will push you to grow and expand your comfort zone. When you reach those goals, you'll prove to yourself that you're capable of more than you ever thought possible. That's what we call KICKASS self-belief!

C. Surround Yourself With KICKASS People: Ditch the naysayers and toxic influences in your life. Instead, surround yourself with people who believe in you, support you, and challenge you to be your best self. They'll help you develop that unshakable self-belief that's oh-so-KICKASS.

D. Embrace Your KICKASS Strengths: Identify your unique strengths and talents, and use them to your advantage. When you focus on what you're good at, you'll build confidence in your abilities and strengthen your self-belief. Remember, being KICKASS means owning your strengths and using them to change the world!

E. Don't Fear Failure: Fear of failure can cripple your self-belief. But guess what? Failure is just a part of the journey. Instead of fearing it, embrace it as an opportunity to learn, grow, and come back stronger than ever. As the legendary Michael Jordan once said, "I've failed over and over and over again in my life. And that is why I succeed." So, be like Mike and turn your failures into KICKASS success stories!

Now, you're well on your way to developing that unshakable self-belief that will serve as the rock-solid foundation for your self-confidence. But we're just getting started! Stay tuned for the next section, "The Confidence-Action Loop," where we'll explore how taking action can boost your confidence and create a positive feedback loop that will propel you toward even greater KICKASS achievements.

Section 2: The Confidence-Action Loop: How taking action can boost your confidence and create a positive feedback loop.

Welcome to the next KICKASS section of this chapter! We're about to dive into the Confidence-Action Loop, which is a game-changer when it comes to building bulletproof confidence. Let's jump right in!

The Confidence-Action Loop is a simple but powerful concept: taking action boosts your confidence, and increased confidence leads to more action. It's a positive feedback loop that feeds on itself, creating a KICKASS upward spiral of confidence and achievement. So, how do we jump-start this loop and make it work for us? Here are some KICKASS steps to get you started:

A. Take the First Step: Sometimes, the hardest part is just getting started. Don't let fear or doubt hold you back. Remember, "A journey of a thousand miles begins with a single step" (Lao Tzu). Take that first KICKASS step and watch your confidence grow.

B. Build Momentum: Once you've taken the first step, keep the momentum going. Break your goals down into smaller, manageable tasks, and tackle them one by one. As you see progress and rack up small wins, your confidence will skyrocket, and you'll be ready for bigger and bolder KICKASS challenges.

C. Track Your Progress: Keep a record of your achievements, no matter how small. Tracking your progress will help you see how far you've come and serve as a reminder that you're capable of KICKASS things. Plus, it'll give you a confidence boost when you need it most.

D. Embrace Challenges: Push yourself out of your comfort zone and take on challenges that stretch your capabilities. As you overcome obstacles and achieve what once seemed impossible, your confidence will grow, and you'll be more prepared to tackle even bigger KICKASS challenges.

E. Learn from Failure: Remember, failure is just a stepping stone on the path to success. When you stumble, learn from your mistakes, and use them as fuel to come back stronger and more determined than ever. That's the KICKASS way to turn failure into confidence!

F. Celebrate Your Successes: Don't forget to celebrate your victories, both big and small. Acknowledging your achievements reinforces your self-belief and fuels your confidence, making you ready to conquer the next KICKASS challenge.

Now that you've got a handle on the Confidence-Action Loop, you're well on your way to building bulletproof confidence. Keep pushing yourself, taking action, and embracing challenges, and watch your confidence soar to new KICKASS heights.

Up next, we'll dive into "Owning Your Success," where we'll explore the importance of celebrating your achievements and giving yourself the credit you deserve.

Section 3: Owning Your Success: Celebrating your achievements and giving yourself the credit you deserve.

Alright, you KICKASS confidence-builder, it's time for the next section: Owning Your Success. We'll be focusing on celebrating your achievements and giving yourself the credit you deserve. Let's dive right in!

Owning your success is all about acknowledging your accomplishments, no matter how big or small, and recognizing the hard work and dedication that got you there. It's about being proud of what you've achieved and using that pride to fuel your confidence and self-belief. So, how can you own your success like a KICKASS champion? Here are some tips:

A. Keep a Brag File: Create a dedicated space (a journal, a folder, or even a digital document) where you can record your achievements, milestones, and KICKASS moments. This "brag file" will serve as a constant reminder of your accomplishments and provide a confidence boost whenever you need it.

B. Share Your Success: Don't be shy about sharing your achievements with others. Celebrate your wins with friends, family, and colleagues. Not only will this reinforce your self-belief, but it'll also inspire others to chase their own KICKASS dreams.

C. Practice Gratitude: Take time to reflect on your accomplishments and express gratitude for the opportunities, resources, and support that have contributed to your success. This will help you maintain a positive mindset and strengthen your confidence even further.

D. Give Credit Where It's Due: Acknowledge the role you played in your achievements. Don't downplay your hard work, talent, or determination. Be proud of your contributions and own your success like the KICKASS individual you are!

E. Reward Yourself: Celebrate your victories by rewarding yourself with something you enjoy, whether it's a special treat, a day off, or a new experience. This positive reinforcement will motivate you to keep pushing forward and achieving even greater KICKASS feats.

F. Set New Goals: As you achieve your goals and own your success, it's essential to set new, more challenging objectives. This will keep you moving forward, growing, and building on your existing KICKASS confidence.

By owning your success, you'll reinforce your self-belief and build even stronger, more bulletproof confidence. Remember, you've earned your achievements, and you deserve to be proud of them! Keep celebrating your victories, giving yourself credit, and pursuing new KICKASS goals.

Now, prepare yourself for the final section of this chapter, "The Charisma Factor," where we'll explore how to cultivate the magnetic presence that comes with authentic confidence. Get ready for some more KICKASS content!

Section 4: The Charisma Factor: Cultivating the magnetic presence that comes with authentic confidence.

Get ready for the grand finale of this KICKASS chapter on building bulletproof confidence! In this final section, we're going to explore the Charisma Factor – the magnetic presence that comes with authentic confidence. Let's jump right in!

Charisma is that captivating, irresistible quality that draws people to you like a moth to a flame. It's the secret sauce that sets KICKASS leaders, influencers, and achievers apart from the rest. And guess what? With bulletproof confidence, you can cultivate your own unique brand of charisma! Here's how:

A. Be Present: When you're fully present in the moment, you exude a magnetic energy that draws people in. Practice active listening, maintain eye contact, and engage fully in conversations. By being genuinely present, you'll radiate KICKASS charisma.

B. Express Yourself Authentically: Authenticity is the foundation of charisma. Be true to yourself, share your thoughts and feelings openly, and don't be afraid to show vulnerability. Embracing your authentic self will make you more relatable, trustworthy, and undeniably KICKASS.

C. Show Genuine Interest in Others: People are drawn to those who take a genuine interest in them. Ask questions, listen attentively, and engage in meaningful conversations. By showing sincere interest in others, you'll cultivate KICKASS connections and strengthen your charisma.

D. Use Positive Body Language: Your body language speaks volumes. Stand tall, maintain an open posture, and use expressive gestures to communicate confidence and enthusiasm. This KICKASS body language will amplify your charisma and make you more approachable.

E. Be Passionate: Passion is infectious! When you're passionate about something, your enthusiasm and energy become irresistibly attractive. Share your passions with others and watch as your charisma factor goes through the roof.

F. Cultivate a Sense of Humor: Laughter is a powerful connector. A well-timed joke or a witty remark can break the ice and build rapport. Don't take yourself too seriously, and use humor to showcase your KICKASS charisma.

G. Practice Empathy: Put yourself in others' shoes and strive to understand their perspectives, feelings, and experiences. This empathetic approach will make you more compassionate, relatable, and undeniably charismatic.

By cultivating the Charisma Factor, you'll not only strengthen your bulletproof confidence but also develop a magnetic presence that attracts success, opportunities, and KICKASS relationships. Remember, authentic confidence is the key to unlocking your full charismatic potential.

And with that, we've reached the end of this KICKASS chapter on building bulletproof confidence! Keep working on your unshakable self-belief, mastering the Confidence-Action Loop, owning your success, and cultivating your Charisma Factor. With dedication and persistence, you'll become a KICKASS powerhouse of confidence, ready to conquer the world!

BONUS CONTENT: The KICKASS Confidence Toolkit

Before we wrap up this chapter, let's dive into some bonus content – a KICKASS Confidence Toolkit to supercharge your journey to bulletproof confidence. These tools and strategies will help you stay on track and make the most of everything you've learned in this chapter.

1. Visualization: Picture yourself succeeding in your mind's eye. Visualize your goals, accomplishments, and the confident, charismatic person you aspire to be. This mental rehearsal will prime your brain for KICKASS success.

2. Affirmations: Develop a set of powerful, positive affirmations that resonate with you. Repeat them daily to reinforce your self-belief and boost your confidence. Examples include: "I am confident and capable," "I embrace challenges and grow stronger," and "I am a KICKASS achiever."

3. Power Poses: Strike a confident pose, such as standing with your hands on your hips or raising your arms in a victory stance. Hold these power poses for a few minutes each day to increase your self-assurance and unleash your KICKASS charisma.

4. Surround Yourself with Support: Build a network of positive, like-minded individuals who believe in you and your KICKASS potential. Their encouragement and support will help you maintain your momentum and confidence on your journey.

5. Develop New Skills: Continuously invest in yourself by learning and mastering new skills. This will not only boost your confidence but also make you a more well-rounded, versatile, and KICKASS individual.

Chapter 13 Summary:

In this KICKASS chapter, we explored:

1. Unshakable Self-Belief: Building a rock-solid foundation of self-confidence

2. The Confidence-Action Loop: Taking action to boost confidence and create a positive feedback loop

3. Owning Your Success: Celebrating achievements and giving yourself the credit you deserve

4. The Charisma Factor: Cultivating a magnetic presence with authentic confidence

Five KICKASS Questions to Reflect on:

Reflect on your journey with these five questions:

1. What specific steps can you take to develop unshakable self-belief?
2. How can you apply the Confidence-Action Loop in your life to create a positive feedback loop of confidence and action?
3. What strategies will you use to own your success and give yourself the credit you deserve?
4. How will you work on cultivating your unique brand of charisma?
5. Which tools from the KICKASS Confidence Toolkit will you incorporate into your daily routine?

Keep these questions in mind as you move forward on your journey to building bulletproof confidence. Remember, you've got the power to become a KICKASS, confident, and charismatic individual!

Chapter 14: The Joy of Discomfort

Section 1: The Comfort Zone Trap: Understanding the limitations of staying in your comfort zone

What's the one thing that can hold you back more than anything else in this world? You guessed it — it's your f*cking comfort zone! KICKASS individuals know that they need to break free from that cozy, warm trap in order to make real progress in life. Let's dive into what the comfort zone is all about and how you can bust out of it like a f*cking superhero.

So what is the comfort zone? It's that place where everything feels familiar, easy, and risk-free. It's like your own personal cocoon, where you feel safe and protected from the outside world. You might be thinking, "Hey, that doesn't sound so bad!" But the problem is, when you're living in your comfort zone, you're not growing or evolving. You're just stagnating, like a puddle of water that never gets any deeper or wider.

Now, let's get one thing straight: there's nothing inherently wrong with being comfortable. Hell, we all need a little comfort in our lives, especially during tough times. But when comfort becomes your default mode, you're setting yourself up for a life of mediocrity and missed opportunities. As the great American author Mark Twain once said, "Twenty years from now, you will be more disappointed by the things you didn't do than by the ones you did do."

The comfort zone trap is sneaky, insidious, and can creep up on you when you least expect it. One day, you're crushing it at work, taking on new projects, and pushing yourself to learn new skills. The next day, you're coasting along, doing the same old shit day in and day out. Before you know it, you're stuck in a rut, and it's a hell of a lot harder to get out of it than you might think.

But don't worry, my kickass friend, I'm here to help you break free from that godforsaken comfort zone once and for all. First, you need to recognize the signs that you're stuck in the trap:

- You're bored and unfulfilled in your job, relationships, or hobbies.

- You avoid new experiences or challenges like the plague.

- You're terrified of failure, so you stick to what you know you can do well.

- You make excuses for why you can't take risks or try new things.

If any of these signs sound familiar, it's time to wake the f*ck up and start taking control of your life. Don't let fear, complacency, or laziness keep you from becoming the absolute KICKASS version of yourself that you're meant to be.

Here's a simple but powerful exercise to help you bust out of the comfort zone trap:

1. Make a list of all the things you've been avoiding or putting off because they're outside of your comfort zone. This could be anything from signing up for a

public speaking class to joining a new social group or asking your crush out on a date.

2. Prioritize your list based on what scares you the most, with the most terrifying item at the top.

3. Commit to tackling one item on your list every week or month, starting with the scariest one. Don't give yourself any excuses — just f*cking do it.

As you work your way through this exercise, you'll start to realize that the things you once feared aren't so scary after all. In fact, they might even be exhilarating and life-changing. The more you push yourself out of your comfort zone, the more you'll grow, evolve, and become the KICKASS person you were always meant to be. Trust me, once you start stepping out of your comfort zone and embracing the unknown, you'll never look back. You'll start seeking out new challenges and experiences like a f*cking adrenaline junkie, and your life will become more exciting and fulfilling than you ever thought possible.

Remember, my friend, the magic happens outside of your comfort zone. It's where you'll discover your true potential and unleash the KICKASS version of yourself that's been hiding deep within you all along. So go ahead, take a leap of faith, and watch your world expand in ways you never imagined.

Get ready to say goodbye to your old, boring, comfortable life, and say hello to a life that's filled with adventure, growth, and endless possibilities. Be bold, be brave, and most importantly, be KICKASS!

Section 2: The Growth-Pain Connection: How discomfort can lead to personal growth and transformation.

Listen up, because I'm about to drop some serious knowledge on you: growth and pain go hand in hand, like peanut butter and jelly, Batman and Robin, or tequila and bad decisions. If you want to become the most KICKASS version of yourself, you need to embrace the discomfort that comes with pushing your limits and stepping into the unknown. It might hurt like hell at first, but trust me, the payoff is worth every ounce of sweat, blood, and tears.

Why is pain such an integral part of the growth process? It's simple, really: when we're faced with challenges or adversity, we're forced to adapt and evolve in order to overcome them. It's like a muscle that grows stronger after being broken down and rebuilt through intense exercise. Without pain, there's no growth — only stagnation and mediocrity.

But how exactly does discomfort lead to personal growth and transformation? Let's break it down:

1. Discomfort forces you to confront your fears and weaknesses. When you're faced with a challenging situation, you have no choice but to confront the things that scare you the most. By doing so, you'll gain a better understanding of your own limitations and learn how to overcome them.

2. Discomfort builds resilience and mental toughness. Each time you push through the pain and come out the other side, you're proving to yourself that you're stronger than you thought. This builds mental fortitude and resilience, which will serve you well in all areas of your life.

3. Discomfort promotes self-reflection and introspection. When you're in the throes of discomfort, you're forced to dig deep and examine your thoughts, feelings, and motivations. This process of self-reflection can lead to profound personal insights and revelations, helping you grow as a person.

4. Discomfort expands your horizons and broadens your perspective. As you face new challenges and experiences, you'll gain a greater understanding of the world around you and your place in it. This broader perspective will help you approach life with more wisdom and empathy.

Now that you understand the growth-pain connection, it's time to put it into practice. Here are a few KICKASS exercises to help you embrace discomfort and unleash your full potential:

1. Set a goal that scares the shit out of you. Whether it's running a marathon, starting your own business, or traveling solo around the world, choose something that pushes you way out of your comfort zone. The more daunting, the better.

2. Practice "discomfort challenges" on a regular basis. These can be small, everyday tasks like taking cold showers, eating a food you dislike, or striking up a conversation with a stranger. The goal is to train your mind and body to become comfortable with discomfort.

3. Keep a "growth journal" to track your progress and reflect on your experiences. Write down your thoughts, feelings, and insights as you push through discomfort and face new challenges. This will help you gain a deeper understanding of your personal growth journey and keep you motivated to continue pushing your limits.

Remember, my friend, pain is temporary, but growth is forever. Embrace the discomfort, and watch as your life transforms into a KICKASS adventure full of endless possibilities. You've got this!

Section 3: Becoming Comfortable with Discomfort: Embracing new challenges and pushing your boundaries.

Alright, let's get real for a moment: becoming comfortable with discomfort is no walk in the park. It takes courage, determination, and a whole lot of KICKASS attitude. But the good news is, the more you practice leaning into the discomfort, the easier it becomes. Soon, you'll be a f*cking master of embracing challenges and pushing your boundaries like a fearless warrior. So how do you get there? Let's dive in.

1. Cultivate a growth mindset: The first step in becoming comfortable with discomfort is adopting a growth

mindset. This means viewing challenges and setbacks as opportunities for growth and learning, rather than reasons to give up or feel defeated. When you approach life with a growth mindset, you'll be more likely to persevere through tough times and come out stronger on the other side.

2. Reframe your perspective on discomfort: Instead of seeing discomfort as something to be avoided at all costs, try viewing it as a necessary part of the growth process. Remember, without discomfort, there's no growth or progress. By shifting your perspective in this way, you'll be more likely to embrace discomfort and push through it, rather than running away from it.

3. Practice mindfulness and self-compassion: When you're faced with a challenging situation, it's easy to get caught up in negative thoughts and emotions. To counteract this, practice mindfulness by staying present and focusing on your breath. At the same time, practice self-compassion by reminding yourself that it's okay to feel uncomfortable or scared – it's all part of the growth process.

4. Break your goals into manageable steps: Sometimes, the thought of facing a huge challenge can be overwhelming and paralyzing. To make it more manageable, break your goal down into smaller, achievable steps. This will help you build momentum

and confidence as you work towards your ultimate objective.

5. Surround yourself with KICKASS people: One of the best ways to become more comfortable with discomfort is to surround yourself with people who embody the KICKASS attitude you're striving for. These individuals will inspire you, support you, and push you to be your best, no matter how uncomfortable it gets.

6. Celebrate your victories, both big and small: Finally, don't forget to celebrate your successes along the way. Every time you step out of your comfort zone and face a challenge head-on, you're proving to yourself that you're capable of growth and transformation. Take a moment to acknowledge and celebrate these victories – they're a testament to your KICKASS spirit.

The more you practice becoming comfortable with discomfort, the more resilient, courageous, and KICKASS you'll become. Embrace the challenges that life throws your way, and you'll be well on your way to becoming the unstoppable force you were always meant to be.

Section 4: The Reward of Resilience: Building mental toughness and resilience through overcoming adversity.

You've made it this far, my KICKASS friend, and now it's time to talk about one of the most important benefits of embracing discomfort: resilience. Mental toughness and resilience are like the secret sauce that allows you to bounce back from setbacks, face challenges head-on, and keep pushing forward, no matter how tough the going gets. So let's dive into how overcoming adversity can help you build that rock-solid resilience and become an unstoppable force in your life.

1. Embrace failure as a learning opportunity: Nobody likes to fail, but the truth is, failure is an essential part of the growth process. When you embrace failure as an opportunity to learn, grow, and improve, you're building resilience and mental toughness. Each time you fail, you're one step closer to success, so don't be afraid to take risks and make mistakes – it's all part of the journey.

2. Develop a strong support system: It's no secret that overcoming adversity is a hell of a lot easier when you've got a solid support system behind you. Surround yourself with friends, family, and mentors who believe in you, encourage you, and are there to help you pick up the pieces when things don't go as planned. With the right people by your side, you'll feel more confident and resilient in the face of adversity.

3. Practice gratitude and focus on the positives: When shit hits the fan, it's easy to get caught up in negativity and self-pity. But by practicing gratitude and focusing on the positive aspects of your life, you can build resilience and maintain a more optimistic outlook, even during the toughest of times. Remember, there's always a silver lining – you just have to be willing to look for it.

4. Learn to cope with stress and adversity: Developing healthy coping mechanisms is a crucial part of building resilience. This could involve regular exercise, meditation, journaling, or any other activity that helps you manage stress and maintain a sense of balance in your life. By learning to cope effectively with adversity, you'll be better equipped to handle whatever challenges come your way.

5. Cultivate self-confidence and belief in your abilities: The more you believe in yourself and your ability to overcome adversity, the more resilient you'll become. To build self-confidence, focus on your strengths, celebrate your achievements, and remind yourself of your past successes, no matter how small they may seem. The more you believe in your own KICKASS potential, the more unstoppable you'll become.

6. Keep pushing forward, no matter what: Finally, building resilience is all about perseverance and determination. When the going gets tough, the tough get going, and that's exactly what you need to do if you want to develop that rock-solid mental toughness. Don't give up, don't back down, and keep pushing forward, no matter how difficult things may seem. Remember, every challenge is an opportunity to grow, learn, and become even more KICKASS than you were before.

By building resilience and mental toughness through overcoming adversity, you'll become a force to be reckoned with in your life. Challenges will no longer seem insurmountable, and setbacks will simply be stepping stones on your path to greatness. So go out there, embrace discomfort, and become the KICKASS, resilient person you were always meant to be!

Alright, let's wrap up this KICKASS Chapter 14 with some bonus content and a summary that'll blow your mind. And of course, I won't leave you hanging without some KICKASS thought-provoking questions to ponder.

Bonus Content: The Discomfort Challenge – 30 Days to a KICKASS, Resilient You

Ready to put everything you've learned in Chapter 14 into practice? Take on this 30-day Discomfort Challenge to build resilience, step out of your comfort zone, and become the KICKASS person you were always meant to be. Each day, complete a new challenge designed to push your boundaries and help you grow. By the end of the month, you'll be a master of embracing discomfort and overcoming adversity like a true KICKASS warrior.

Summary of Chapter 14:

In Chapter 14, we explored the joy of discomfort and how it's essential for personal growth and transformation. We discussed:

1. The Comfort Zone Trap: Understanding the limitations of staying in your comfort zone, and how breaking free can lead to a more fulfilling and adventurous life.

2. The Growth-Pain Connection: How discomfort and pain are crucial for personal growth and transformation, and the importance of embracing challenges and adversity.

3. Becoming Comfortable with Discomfort: Strategies for embracing new challenges, pushing your boundaries, and cultivating a growth mindset.

4. The Reward of Resilience: Building mental toughness and resilience through overcoming adversity, and how this can help you become an unstoppable force in your life.

Five KICKASS Questions to Reflect on:

1. What is one area of your life where you've been stuck in your comfort zone, and what steps can you take to break free and embrace discomfort?

2. Share a time when you faced adversity and came out stronger because of it. What did you learn from this experience, and how has it helped you grow as a person?

3. What are some daily habits or practices you can implement to help you become more comfortable with discomfort and build resilience?

4. How has your perspective on failure and setbacks changed after reading this chapter? How will you approach future challenges with a growth mindset?

5. Which part of the 30-day Discomfort Challenge are you most excited about, and why? How do you think this challenge will help you become a more KICKASS, resilient person?

There you have it, my KICKASS friend! Chapter 14 packed with insights, strategies, and a bonus 30-day challenge that'll have you embracing discomfort, building resilience, and living your most badass life. Go forth and conquer!

Chapter 15: The Life-Changing Power of Habits

Section 1: Habit Hacking: How to build powerful habits that lead to success and happiness.

Welcome, my kickass friend, to the world of habit hacking! This is where we dive deep into the trenches of our daily routines, get our hands dirty, and come out victorious, armed with powerful habits that will catapult us towards success and happiness.

You're not here for some half-baked, wishy-washy approach to habit formation. No, you want to MAKE IT KICKASS, and that's precisely what we're going to do. Buckle up, because we're about to embark on one hell of a ride.

First, let's define what a habit is. A habit is a pattern of behavior that we perform repeatedly, often unconsciously. It's like a well-trodden path in our brain that we take without even thinking. Now, we want to turn that path into a friggin' superhighway to success.

So, how do we hack our habits? It all starts with understanding the power of consistency. Legendary basketball coach John Wooden once said, "Don't let what you cannot do interfere with what you can do." This kickass quote is the essence of habit hacking – focusing on what we can do and doing it consistently.

Here are some no-nonsense, kickass steps to help you build powerful habits that lead to success and happiness:

1. Define your kickass goals

First, you need to know what you want. Your habits should be aligned with your goals – the more kickass your goals, the more kickass your habits need to be. So, take a moment to list down your wildest dreams and aspirations – and be specific!

2. Start small, but think big

Rome wasn't built in a day, and neither are habits. Start with small, manageable steps that will eventually lead to significant changes. As the saying goes, "The journey of a thousand miles begins with a single step." Just make sure that step is kickass!

3. Make it fun

Who said building habits should be a chore? Turn it into a game, challenge yourself, or team up with friends. The more enjoyable the process, the more likely you are to stick with it. Remember, "The only way to do great work is to love what you do." – Steve Jobs

4. Keep track of your progress

You can't improve what you don't measure. Monitor your progress and celebrate your small victories. This will keep you motivated and help you stay on track. As Peter Drucker said, "What gets measured, gets managed."

5. Build a support system

Surround yourself with like-minded people who share your goals and values. They'll be your rock when the going gets tough and your cheerleaders when you need that extra push. As the legendary Jim Rohn said, "You are the average of the five people you spend the most time with."

6. Embrace setbacks and learn from them

Setbacks are inevitable, but they're also valuable learning experiences. Don't get discouraged when things don't go as planned. Instead, analyze what went wrong, adjust your approach, and keep moving forward. As Thomas Edison said, "I have not failed. I've just found 10,000 ways that won't work."

Now that you have a solid understanding of habit hacking, it's time to put these kickass principles into action. Remember, the key is to be consistent, persistent, and most importantly, enjoy the process. You're building a foundation for a lifetime of success and happiness, so make it count!

Section 2: The Keystone Habits: Identifying the habits that have the greatest impact on your life.

Now that you're all fired up about habit hacking, let's dive into the keystone habits. These are the habits that act as the linchpin of your personal growth and success. They're the ones that, when mastered, will have a profound and transformative impact on your life. So, without further ado, let's MAKE THIS KICKASS section absolutely KICKASS!

1. Exercise: Flex your muscles and your mind

Not only does regular exercise have incredible physical benefits, but it also boosts your mental and emotional well-being. It's the ultimate keystone habit that improves your energy levels, self-confidence, and productivity. As the great Arnold Schwarzenegger once said, "Strength does not come from winning. Your struggles develop your strengths. When you go through hardships and decide not to surrender, that is strength."

2. Sleep: The secret weapon for peak performance
Skimping on sleep is a recipe for disaster. Prioritizing quality sleep will improve your mood, memory, and cognitive function, making it an essential keystone habit. As Arianna Huffington puts it, "Sleep your way to the top." And no, she doesn't mean it that way – get your mind out of the gutter!

3. Nutrition: Fuel your body with the good stuff
You are what you eat, so make sure you're fueling your body with the right nutrients. A balanced, healthy diet will provide you with the energy and mental clarity needed to conquer your goals. As Hippocrates said, "Let food be thy medicine and medicine be thy food."

4. Mindfulness: Stay present and focused
Practicing mindfulness – through meditation, journaling, or other techniques – helps you stay grounded and focused. It increases self-awareness, reduces stress, and enhances emotional intelligence. As the Buddha said, "Do not dwell in the past, do not dream of the future, concentrate the mind on the present moment."

5. Continuous learning: Never stop growing
Knowledge is power, and the most successful people never stop learning. Make it a habit to read, take courses, or attend workshops to expand your mind and stay ahead of the curve. As the legendary Albert Einstein said, "Once you stop learning, you start dying."

6. Gratitude: Appreciate the good things in life

Cultivating an attitude of gratitude will transform your outlook on life. It'll make you more resilient, improve your relationships, and boost your overall happiness. As Oprah Winfrey said, "Be thankful for what you have; you'll end up having more. If you concentrate on what you don't have, you will never, ever have enough."

Now that you know the keystone habits that have the greatest impact on your life, it's time to put them into practice. Remember, the key is to start small and stay consistent. And most importantly, enjoy the process — this is your kickass journey towards personal growth and success!

Section 3: The Habit Loop: Understanding the science behind habit formation and change.

Now that you're familiar with habit hacking and keystone habits, it's time to dive into the nitty-gritty of how habits actually work. Welcome to the Habit Loop — the kickass science behind habit formation and change!

The Habit Loop is a concept developed by Charles Duhigg in his book "The Power of Habit." It breaks down the habit formation process into three distinct stages: Cue, Routine, and Reward. By understanding how these stages work, you'll be better equipped to create kickass new habits and change the not-so-kickass ones.

1. Cue

The cue is the trigger that initiates the habit. It can be a specific time, location, emotional state, or even the presence of other people. For example, your morning alarm (cue) might prompt you to jump out of bed and start your daily workout routine.

2. Routine

The routine is the actual behavior or action you perform in response to the cue. In our example, the routine is the workout you engage in after hearing the alarm. This is the heart of the habit, and it's where the magic (or the kickassery) happens!

3. Reward

The reward is the positive outcome or benefit you receive from performing the routine. In the case of our example, the reward might be the endorphin rush, sense of accomplishment, or improved physical fitness you experience after completing your workout.

Now that you understand the Habit Loop, it's time to put this knowledge into action. Here are some kickass tips for using the Habit Loop to create and change habits:

4. Identify your cues

To create a new habit or change an existing one, you need to be aware of the cues that trigger the routine. Take note of the specific circumstances that prompt your behavior and use this information to your advantage.

5. Modify your routine

Once you've identified the cue, you can focus on changing the routine. If you're trying to create a new habit, develop a kickass routine that aligns with your goals. If you're working on breaking a bad habit, replace the negative routine with a more positive one.

6. Make the reward irresistible

An essential part of habit formation is ensuring the reward is enticing enough to motivate you to perform the routine consistently. Find a reward that genuinely excites and motivates you – it could be something as simple as a small treat, praise from a friend, or the satisfaction of ticking an item off your to-do list.

By leveraging the power of the Habit Loop, you'll be well on your way to creating kickass habits that stick. Remember, habit formation is a process, and change takes time. Be patient, stay consistent, and most importantly, enjoy the journey towards a more KICKASS, successful, and happier life.

Section 4: Breaking Bad: Strategies for replacing negative habits with positive ones.

Alright, my kickass friend, it's time to face the final boss – breaking those pesky negative habits and replacing them with powerful, life-changing positive ones. This section is all about giving your habits a complete makeover – from bad to kickass!

Now that you understand the Habit Loop, you have the knowledge and tools to tackle even the most stubborn habits. But, let's not sugarcoat it – change is tough. So, buckle up and get ready to kick some bad habit ass with these kickass strategies:

1. Take it one habit at a time

Don't try to overhaul your entire life overnight. Focus on one habit at a time and give it your undivided attention. As Bruce Lee said, "I fear not the man who has practiced 10,000 kicks once, but I fear the man who has practiced one kick 10,000 times."

2. Use the Habit Loop to your advantage

Remember the Habit Loop? It's time to put it into action. Identify the cues that trigger your bad habits and use them as a springboard to kickstart your positive routines. Then, make sure the reward is so enticing that you can't help but crave it.

3. Set up your environment for success

You know what they say, "Out of sight, out of mind." Remove temptations and triggers from your environment, and make it as easy as possible for you to perform your new, positive routines. Set yourself up for kickass success!

4. Make a public commitment

Share your goals and intentions with friends, family, or even social media. Making a public commitment adds an extra layer of accountability, which can help keep you on track when the going gets tough. Besides, who doesn't love a little cheering section?

5. Practice patience and perseverance

Breaking bad habits and replacing them with positive ones takes time, effort, and patience. Remember that setbacks are part of the process, and it's essential to keep pushing forward. As Winston Churchill said, "Success is not final, failure is not fatal: It is the courage to continue that counts."

6. Celebrate your victories, big and small

Don't forget to reward yourself for your progress and accomplishments. Celebrate the small wins along the way and use them as motivation to keep pushing forward. As the legendary Oprah Winfrey said, "The more you praise and celebrate your life, the more there is in life to celebrate."

By implementing these kickass strategies, you'll be well on your way to breaking free from the shackles of negative habits and embracing a life filled with positivity, success, and happiness. Just remember, change doesn't happen overnight — it takes time, effort, and dedication. But with the right mindset and tools in your arsenal, you can conquer even the most stubborn habits and unleash your true kickass potential.

Kickass Bonus Content: The Power of Habit Tracking

Before we wrap up this life-changing chapter, let's dive into some bonus content — habit tracking. Tracking your habits is a powerful tool that helps keep you accountable, measure progress, and maintain motivation. By consistently monitoring your habits, you'll become more aware of your actions and their impact on your life. So, let's explore some kickass ways to track your habits:

- Use a habit-tracking app: There are plenty of apps available that make habit tracking a breeze. Some popular options include Habitica, Streaks, and HabitBull. Choose one that resonates with you and start tracking!

- Create a habit tracker in your journal: If you prefer a more analog approach, grab a pen and paper and create a habit tracker in your journal. Customize it to suit your needs and make it visually appealing to keep you motivated.

- Use a wall calendar: A wall calendar is a simple and effective way to track your habits. Just mark off each day you complete your habit, and watch your progress unfold before your eyes.

Now that we've covered some bonus content, let's wrap up this kickass chapter with a summary and five thought-provoking questions:

Chapter 15 Summary:

1. Habit Hacking: Build powerful habits that lead to success and happiness.

2. The Keystone Habits: Identify the habits that have the most significant impact on your life.

3. The Habit Loop: Understand the science behind habit formation and change.

4. Breaking Bad: Replace negative habits with positive ones using kickass strategies.

Five KICKASS Questions to Reflect on:

1. Which keystone habits could have the biggest impact on your life, and how can you start implementing them?

2. How can you modify the Habit Loop to replace a negative habit with a positive one?

3. What strategies from the "Breaking Bad" section resonate most with you, and how can you use them to conquer your negative habits?

4. How can you set up your environment to promote positive habits and discourage negative ones?

5. Which habit-tracking method will work best for you, and how can you implement it to ensure consistent progress?

Keep these questions in mind as you continue on your journey to building kickass habits that lead to a life of success and happiness. Remember, change takes time, effort, and dedication – but with the right tools and mindset, there's nothing you can't achieve!

Chapter 16: The Pursuit of Passion

Section 1: Igniting the Fire Within: Discovering your passions and finding your true calling

Let me tell you something, my friend. Life is too short to be living someone else's dream. You've got to find what sets your soul on fire and make it your life's mission. That's where the magic happens, and that's what we're going to explore in this KICKASS section. So, buckle up and get ready for a wild ride, as we learn how to ignite the fire within, discover our passions, and find our true calling.

The first thing you need to understand is that passion is not a one-size-fits-all concept. It's unique to every individual, just like a fingerprint. Your passion might be painting, dancing, writing, or even collecting vintage teapots. Whatever it is, it's yours, and that's what makes it special.

Now, you might be thinking, "But Mickey, how do I find my passion?" Well, I'm glad you asked. Here are some KICKASS steps to help you ignite the fire within and discover what you're truly passionate about:

1. Explore and Experiment

Life is a smorgasbord of experiences, and you've got to taste as much as you can. Try out new hobbies, attend workshops, join clubs, or volunteer. The more you expose yourself to different experiences, the higher your chances of finding something that ignites your passion.

2. Reflect on Your Life

Think back to the moments in your life when you felt most alive and excited. What were you doing? Who were you with? Analyze these moments to find clues about your passions.

3. Ask Yourself the Right Questions

Sometimes, all it takes to find your passion is asking yourself the right questions. Here are a few to get you started:

- What activities make me lose track of time?
- If I had all the money in the world, what would I do with my time?
- What do I love talking about or teaching others?

4. Look for Patterns

As you explore, reflect, and ask yourself questions, you'll start to notice patterns emerging. These patterns will lead you to your passions.

Once you've identified your passions, it's time to find your true calling. Your true calling is the sweet spot where your passion, skills, and the needs of the world intersect. To find this sweet spot, ask yourself these KICKASS questions:

1. What am I good at?

2. What do I love doing?

3. What does the world need?

Remember, your true calling doesn't have to be a conventional career. It could be starting a non-profit, creating art, or even building a sustainable farm. The key is to find something that lights up your soul and brings value to the world.

Now, I want you to do a KICKASS exercise. Grab a pen and paper, and write down your answers to the questions above. Then, spend some time brainstorming how you could merge your passions, skills, and the needs of the world to find your true calling.

To wrap this KICKASS section up, I want to leave you with a quote from the legendary Steve Jobs: "Your work is going to fill a large part of your life, and the only way to be truly satisfied is to do what you believe is great work. And the only way to do great work is to love what you do."

So, my friend, go out there, ignite the fire within, and find your true calling. Your life will never be the same again.

Section 2: The Passion-Drive Connection: How following your passions can fuel your motivation and success

Alright, my friend, now that we've talked about igniting the fire within and finding your true calling, let's dive into how following your passions can fuel your motivation and lead to KICKASS success.

The truth is, when you're passionate about something, you're naturally more motivated, energized, and determined to succeed. Passion is like rocket fuel for your dreams, propelling you forward and pushing you to achieve greater heights. But how does this connection between passion and drive work?

And how can you harness it to crush your goals and create the life you've always wanted? Let's find out.

a. Passion Breeds Motivation: When you're truly passionate about something, it doesn't feel like work. It's fun, exciting, and invigorating. This positive emotional state helps create a feedback loop of motivation that keeps you engaged and focused on your goals.

b. Passion Creates Resilience: Let's be real; life is full of challenges and setbacks. But when you're passionate about something, you're more likely to persevere and overcome obstacles. Passion gives you the grit and resilience needed to bounce back from failure and keep pushing forward.

c. Passion Fuels Creativity: Passionate people are natural innovators. They're always looking for new ways to improve, grow, and make their mark on the world. When you're passionate about something, you're more likely to think outside the box and come up with KICKASS ideas that set you apart from the competition.

d. Passion Builds Confidence: As you pursue your passions and start seeing results, your confidence will soar. You'll begin to believe in yourself and your abilities, and this newfound confidence will spill over into other areas of your life, creating a positive domino effect.

Now that we've explored the passion-drive connection, let's talk about some KICKASS strategies to help you harness this power and create unstoppable momentum:

1. Set SMART Goals: To stay motivated and focused on your passion, set Specific, Measurable, Achievable, Relevant, and Time-bound goals. This will give you a clear roadmap to success and help you track your progress.

2. Surround Yourself with Support: Your environment plays a huge role in your success. Surround yourself with people who share your passions and support your dreams. They'll inspire you, keep you accountable, and help you stay motivated through the ups and downs.

3. Prioritize Self-Care: To keep your passion alive, it's essential to take care of yourself physically, mentally, and emotionally. Make time for exercise, proper nutrition, sleep, and relaxation. A healthy body and mind will give you the energy and focus you need to pursue your passions with full force.

4. Celebrate Your Wins: It's crucial to acknowledge and celebrate your successes, no matter how small. This will boost your motivation, reinforce your positive habits, and help you stay committed to your passion.

So there you have it, my friend – the passion-drive connection and some KICKASS strategies to help you follow your passions, fuel your motivation, and achieve incredible success. Remember, life is too short to settle for mediocrity. Pursue your passions with unrelenting determination, and watch your dreams become a reality.

Section 3: Integrating Passion into Your Life: Creating a lifestyle that supports and nurtures your passions

Alright, you've discovered your passions and found your true calling. Now, it's time to make that KICKASS passion an integral part of your life. Integrating your passion into your life is crucial because when you're living in alignment with your passion, you'll be happier, more fulfilled, and have more energy to take on the world. So, let's dive into some KICKASS strategies for integrating your passion into your life:

1. Create a Passion-Driven Routine: If you want to live a life fueled by your passion, you need to make time for it. Start by carving out dedicated time each day or week to pursue your passion. Block off time in your calendar, set reminders, and treat it like an essential appointment with yourself. Prioritize your passion, and watch it transform your life.

2. Surround Yourself with Inspiration: Your environment plays a huge role in nurturing your passion. Create a space that inspires and supports your passion, whether it's a home office, a studio, or even just a corner of your bedroom. Fill it with objects, quotes, and images that remind you of your passion and keep your creative juices flowing.

3. Connect with Like-Minded People: Sharing your passion with others can be a powerful way to fuel your fire. Seek out people who share your passion, and create a

KICKASS support network. Join clubs, online forums, or attend meet-ups and conferences. The more you immerse yourself in the community, the more inspired and motivated you'll be.

4. Set KICKASS Goals: To keep your passion alive and thriving, it's important to set goals that challenge and excite you. Break your big goals down into smaller, more manageable steps, and celebrate your progress along the way. Remember, your goals should be SMART – Specific, Measurable, Achievable, Relevant, and Time-Bound. This will help you stay on track and maintain your momentum.

5. Embrace Challenges and Learn from Failure: Pursuing your passion won't always be smooth sailing. You'll face obstacles, setbacks, and failures along the way. But remember, failure is just a stepping stone to success. Embrace challenges, learn from your mistakes, and use them to fuel your passion even more.

6. Maintain Balance: While it's important to be passionate and dedicated, it's also crucial to maintain balance in your life. Don't let your passion consume you to the point that you neglect other important aspects of your life like relationships, health, and self-care. Find a balance that allows you to nurture your passion while still maintaining a healthy, well-rounded life.

Now, it's time for a KICKASS exercise. Grab that pen and paper again, and make a list of the changes you can make in your life to better support and nurture your passion. Be as specific as possible, and don't be afraid to think big.

Remember, my friend, integrating your passion into your life is an ongoing process. It takes time, effort, and dedication, but the rewards are worth it. With every step you take towards living a passion-driven life, you'll unlock a new level of happiness, fulfillment, and success.

As the brilliant Maya Angelou once said, "You can only become truly accomplished at something you love. Don't make money your goal. Instead, pursue the things you love doing, and then do them so well that people can't take their eyes off you." Now, go out there and make your passion an integral part of your KICKASS life!

Section 4: The Ripple Effect of Passion: How pursuing your passions can inspire others and make a positive impact on the world

You've discovered your passions, found your true calling, and started integrating them into your life. Now it's time to take it to the next level and explore the KICKASS ripple effect of pursuing your passions. What if I told you that by chasing your dreams and living a passionate life, you can inspire others and make a positive impact on the world? Sounds amazing, right? Well, buckle up because we're about to dive deep into this powerful concept.

When you're passionate about something, it's contagious. People can sense it, and they're drawn to it. They want to be around you, learn from you, and be inspired by your energy. It's like you're a magnet, and your passion is attracting all the good vibes and positive energy around you. This is the beginning of the ripple effect.

As you pursue your passions and start achieving success, you'll notice that people begin to take notice. They'll be curious about what you're doing, how you're doing it, and why you're so damn excited about it. This curiosity will lead them to start exploring their own passions and finding their true callings. You'll be like a spark that ignites the fire within others, and the ripples will keep on expanding.

But the ripple effect doesn't stop there. When you're living a life filled with passion, you're more likely to take risks, challenge the status quo, and push boundaries. You'll be a trailblazer, carving out new paths and showing others that it's possible to live a fulfilling and extraordinary life. This will inspire others to follow in your footsteps, leading to more innovation, creativity, and progress in the world.

The ripple effect of pursuing your passions is also about the impact you can have on the world. When you're passionate about something, you're more likely to give it your all, work hard, and persevere through challenges. This dedication and commitment can lead to remarkable achievements that can positively impact your community, your country, and even the entire world. Think about people like Elon Musk, Malala

Yousafzai, or Jane Goodall - their passion for their work has led to groundbreaking advancements and transformative change in their respective fields.

Now, I want you to do another KICKASS exercise. Take a moment to think about how your passions can create a ripple effect in your life and the lives of others. What impact could your passion have on your community, your country, or the world? Write down your thoughts, and then brainstorm a few ways you can amplify this ripple effect and inspire even more people.

To conclude this KICKASS section, I want to leave you with a quote from the great Oprah Winfrey: "Passion is energy. Feel the power that comes from focusing on what excites you." So, embrace the ripple effect of passion, and watch as your energy and excitement inspire others and make a positive impact on the world. Now go out there, make some waves, and KICKASS!

KICKASS Bonus Content:

Before we jump into the summary, I want to share some KICKASS bonus content to help you supercharge your pursuit of passion. Here are three additional ways to enhance your passion-driven journey:

1. Surround Yourself with Passionate People: You're the average of the five people you spend the most time with, so make sure you're hanging out with KICKASS individuals who share your enthusiasm and drive. Their

energy will fuel your fire and keep you motivated on your journey.

2. Stay Curious: Never stop learning and seeking new experiences. The more you grow and evolve, the more your passions will expand and deepen. Embrace lifelong learning and always strive to become the best version of yourself.

3. Give Back: Use your passion to make a difference in the world. Share your knowledge, skills, and resources with others, and empower them to chase their dreams as well. The more you give, the more fulfillment you'll experience in your own life.

Now, let's wrap up this KICKASS chapter with a summary and five thought-provoking questions.

Summary of Chapter 16: The Pursuit of Passion

1. Igniting the Fire Within: Explore, experiment, and reflect on your life to discover your passions and find your true calling.

2. The Passion-Drive Connection: Passion fuels motivation and success, leading to a fulfilling and extraordinary life.

3. Integrating Passion into Your Life: Create a lifestyle that supports and nurtures your passions, and watch as your life transforms.

4. The Ripple Effect of Passion: Pursuing your passions inspires others, fosters innovation, and makes a positive impact on the world.

Five KICKASS Questions to Reflect on:

1. What is one new experience you can try this week to explore your passions and discover your true calling?

2. How can you integrate your passion into your daily life, even if it's just for a few minutes each day?

3. Who are the passionate people in your life, and how can you spend more time with them to fuel your own fire?

4. In what ways can you give back to others and use your passion to create a positive impact in your community or the world?

5. How can you stay curious and continue learning and growing in your pursuit of passion?

Now it's time to take this KICKASS knowledge and apply it to your life. Embrace your passions, chase your dreams, and watch as the ripple effect of your energy inspires others and transforms the world. Keep it KICKASS, my friend!

Chapter 17: Nurturing Your Mental Health

Section 1: The Mind-Body Connection: Understanding the link between mental health and overall well-being

Let me hit you with some truth: your mental health is KICKASS important! You might be wondering, "Mickey, what the hell does mental health have to do with overall well-being?" Well, buckle up, because I'm about to drop some knowledge bombs. The mind-body connection is no joke – it's the key to unlocking a life that kicks ass in every way possible.

First things first, let's lay down the facts. The mind-body connection is the relationship between your thoughts, feelings, and actions, and how they influence your physical health. Your brain is the central command center of your body, so it's no surprise that what happens up there has a profound impact on your overall well-being.

You've probably heard the saying, "A healthy mind in a healthy body." That's because mental and physical health go hand in hand like PB&J. If one part of the equation is off, you can bet your ass the other will be affected.

Now, let's dive deeper into this mind-body connection. Think about a time when you were stressed out or anxious. How did your body react? Maybe you had a headache, your heart raced, or your muscles were tense. That's your body reacting to your mental state, and it's just one example of how your thoughts and emotions can have a KICKASS impact on your physical health.

But it's not all doom and gloom! The mind-body connection is a two-way street, which means that taking care of your mental health can lead to improvements in your physical health too. So, how do you make the most of this connection? Here are a few tips to help you nurture your mental health and boost your overall well-being:

- Prioritize self-care: Carve out time in your busy schedule for activities that make you feel good, whether it's a bubble bath, a hike, or binge-watching your favorite show. Remember, self-care isn't selfish – it's essential for your mental health!

- Practice mindfulness: Being present and aware of your thoughts, feelings, and bodily sensations can help you tune into your mind-body connection. Try incorporating mindfulness techniques like meditation or deep breathing into your daily routine.

- Get moving: Exercise is a KICKASS way to boost both your mental and physical health. Aim for at least 150 minutes of moderate-intensity aerobic activity each week, plus muscle-strengthening exercises on two or more days.

- Feed your brain: A healthy diet is crucial for a healthy mind. Focus on whole, nutrient-dense foods like fruits, vegetables, whole grains, lean proteins, and healthy fats to keep your brain firing on all cylinders.

- Connect with others: Humans are social creatures, and having strong relationships is essential for mental health. Make time for the people who matter most in your life, and don't be afraid to open up about your thoughts and feelings.

- Laugh it off: Laughter really is the best medicine! Find humor in your everyday life, and don't take yourself too seriously. Laughing not only improves your mood but also strengthens your immune system and relieves stress.

So there you have it — a crash course on the mind-body connection and how it influences your overall well-being. Remember, taking care of your mental health isn't just about feeling good — it's about living a KICKASS life that's bursting with energy, vitality, and purpose. Because at the end of the day, a healthy mind is the key to a healthy body, and a healthy body is the key to a life that kicks some serious ass.

Section 2: Mindful Self-Compassion: Cultivating a kind and caring relationship with yourself

Alright, let's get down to some KICKASS self-compassion! You might think, "Mickey, I don't have time for all that fluffy self-love stuff." But trust me, cultivating a kind and caring relationship with yourself isn't just some new-age mumbo jumbo — it's the secret sauce for achieving a badass, fulfilling life.

So, what the hell is mindful self-compassion? It's all about treating yourself with the same kindness, understanding, and patience that you'd extend to a close friend or family member. Instead of beating yourself up over every little mistake, it's about acknowledging your imperfections and giving yourself a break. It's about recognizing that nobody's perfect, not even you, and that's totally okay.

Ready to give this mindful self-compassion thing a try? Here are some KICKASS tips to help you cultivate a kinder, more caring relationship with yourself:

1. Watch your self-talk: Pay attention to the way you speak to yourself in your head. If you wouldn't say it to a friend, don't say it to yourself. Replace negative thoughts with kinder, more compassionate ones. Remember, you're a KICKASS individual, and you deserve to be treated like one — even by yourself!

2. Practice mindfulness: We've talked about this before, but mindfulness is essential for self-compassion. When you're present and aware of your thoughts and emotions, you're better equipped to respond to them with kindness and understanding. So, take a deep breath, tune into your body, and give yourself the gift of mindfulness.

3. Embrace imperfection: Nobody's perfect, and expecting yourself to be is a one-way ticket to disappointment. Instead, learn to accept your flaws and recognize that they're part of what makes you unique. As the legendary Leonard Cohen once said, "There is a crack in everything. That's how the light gets in."

4. Practice self-forgiveness: When you mess up (and you will, because you're human), don't dwell on your mistakes. Instead, acknowledge them, learn from them, and move on. Remember, you're a work in progress, and every misstep is an opportunity for growth.

5. Treat yourself: Self-compassion isn't just about being kind to yourself in your thoughts – it's also about treating yourself with love and care. So, go ahead and indulge in that bubble bath, buy yourself those shoes you've been eyeing, or take a day off just because. You deserve it!

6. Connect with others: Sharing your struggles with friends or loved ones can help you feel less alone and more understood. Plus, it's a great reminder that everyone faces challenges and that it's okay to be vulnerable.

By embracing mindful self-compassion, you're not only doing yourself a favor – you're also setting yourself up for a more KICKASS life. Because when you're kind and caring toward yourself, you're better equipped to face life's challenges head-on, bounce back from setbacks, and live a life that's truly fulfilling. So, go ahead and give yourself a big ol' hug (literally or metaphorically), because you, my friend, are worth it!

Section 3: Stress-Busting Strategies: Techniques for managing stress and preventing burnout

Let's face it – life can be one hell of a rollercoaster. With deadlines, responsibilities, and curveballs being thrown at us left, right, and center, it's no wonder stress is a constant companion for many of us. But here's the KICKASS truth: you don't have to let stress rule your life. With the right stress-busting strategies in your arsenal, you can manage stress like a pro and prevent burnout before it even has a chance to rear its ugly head. So, without further ado, let's dive into some KICKASS techniques to help you keep stress in check and live your best life!

1. Embrace the power of "no": Repeat after me: "It's okay to say no." You can't do everything for everyone, and overcommitting yourself is a one-way ticket to Stressville. Learn to set boundaries and prioritize your time and energy. Saying no doesn't make you a bad person — it makes you a smart, self-aware individual who knows their limits.

2. Get your Zzzs: A good night's sleep is like a magical elixir for stress. Aim for 7-9 hours of quality shut-eye each night, and watch your stress levels melt away. Establish a bedtime routine, make your sleep environment as cozy as possible, and try relaxation techniques if you're struggling to drift off.

3. Shake it off: When stress strikes, don't just sit there and stew — get up and get moving! Physical activity is a KICKASS stress-buster that releases feel-good endorphins and helps clear your mind. Find an exercise you enjoy, whether it's dancing, running, or practicing yoga, and make it a non-negotiable part of your routine.

4. Talk it out: Don't bottle up your stress – let it out! Sharing your thoughts and feelings with someone you trust can work wonders for your mental health. Whether it's a friend, family member, or therapist, talking through your stressors can help you gain perspective and develop strategies for dealing with them.

5. Chill out with a hobby: When life gets hectic, it's important to have a go-to activity that helps you relax and unwind. Pick up a hobby that brings you joy, like painting, playing an instrument, or gardening, and carve out time for it each week. Your stress levels will thank you!

6. Practice gratitude: Focus on the positive aspects of your life, and you'll be amazed at how much lighter your stress load becomes. Keep a gratitude journal, and jot down three things you're grateful for each day. It's a simple yet KICKASS way to shift your mindset and keep stress at bay.

7. Master the art of deep breathing: When stress rears its head, take a deep breath – literally. Deep breathing exercises can help you calm down and regain control in stressful situations. Try the 4-7-8 technique: inhale for 4 seconds, hold your breath for 7 seconds, and exhale for 8 seconds. Repeat a few times, and feel the stress melt away.

By putting these KICKASS stress-busting strategies into practice, you'll be well on your way to managing stress like a champ and preventing burnout before it has a chance to take hold. Remember, life may be full of ups and downs, but with the right tools and mindset, you can tackle whatever comes your way with confidence and resilience. So go forth and conquer, my friend — the world is your stress-free oyster!

Section 4: Seeking Support: Recognizing when to ask for help and building a strong support network

Listen up, folks! Nobody, and I mean NOBODY, can go through life without needing a little help now and then. No one's expecting you to be a superhero who can handle everything on their own. Life's tough, and sometimes you need a KICKASS support network to get through the rough patches. So, let's talk about recognizing when to ask for help and how to build that strong support network.

First off, let me tell you a secret: asking for help is a sign of strength, not weakness. It takes a lot of courage to admit when you're struggling, and reaching out for support shows that you're committed to getting better. So, how do you know when it's time to ask for help? Here are some signs that it might be time to reach out:

- You're feeling overwhelmed and can't seem to cope with your problems on your own.
- Your thoughts, feelings, or behaviors are negatively impacting your daily life, work, or relationships.
- You're isolating yourself from friends and family.

- You're using unhealthy coping mechanisms like drugs, alcohol, or self-harm.

- You've experienced a traumatic event and can't seem to move past it.

Now that you know when to ask for help let's talk about building that KICKASS support network. A strong support network is like a safety net that catches you when you fall, and it's made up of people who genuinely care about your well-being. Here's how to start building your network:

1. Be open: Let the people in your life know what you're going through. It's okay to be vulnerable – in fact, it's essential for building deep connections. Don't be afraid to share your thoughts and feelings, even if it's scary at first.

2. Choose wisely: Surround yourself with positive, supportive people who lift you up and inspire you to be your best self. Cut ties with the naysayers, the energy vampires, and the toxic relationships that only bring you down.

3. Be a good listener: Building a support network is a two-way street. Show your friends and family that you're there for them too by lending a listening ear when they need it.

4. Join a support group: Sometimes, it helps to connect with others who are going through the same struggles

as you. Look for local or online support groups where you can share your experiences and learn from others.

5. Lean on professionals: Don't hesitate to seek professional help if you need it. A therapist, counselor, or psychiatrist can provide valuable guidance and support on your mental health journey.

6. Cultivate self-support: While a strong support network is crucial, it's also essential to develop your own inner resources for self-support. Practice self-compassion and self-care to foster resilience and emotional well-being.

So, there you have it – the lowdown on seeking support and building a KICKASS support network. Remember, asking for help is a sign of strength, not weakness, and having a strong support network is essential for navigating life's ups and downs. So, go out there and start building those connections – because when the going gets tough, you're going to need some KICKASS people in your corner.

KICKASS Bonus Content: The Power of Positivity

Before we wrap up this chapter, let me hit you with some bonus content – the power of positivity. Maintaining a positive mindset can work wonders for your mental health and overall well-being. When you focus on the good in life and cultivate an attitude of gratitude, you'll find that your problems seem more manageable, and your support network grows even stronger.

So, let's dive into some KICKASS tips for harnessing the power of positivity:

1. Start a gratitude journal: Every day, write down three things you're grateful for. This simple practice can shift your mindset and help you focus on the good in life.

2. Surround yourself with positivity: Choose friends who uplift and inspire you, and fill your environment with positive messages, images, and quotes.

3. Turn negatives into positives: When faced with challenges, look for the silver lining or the lesson to be learned. This can help you reframe your perspective and find the opportunity in adversity.

4. Set realistic goals: Establish achievable goals that push you to grow without setting yourself up for failure. Break them down into smaller steps and celebrate your progress along the way.

5. Practice positive self-talk: Be mindful of the way you talk to yourself, and replace negative thoughts with positive affirmations. Remember, you're your own biggest cheerleader!

Summary of Chapter 17: Nurturing Your Mental Health

In this KICKASS chapter, we explored the importance of nurturing your mental health for a well-balanced life. We delved into the mind-body connection and discovered how mental health influences overall well-being. We discussed the importance of mindful self-compassion and shared stress-busting strategies for managing daily pressures. Finally, we looked at the significance of seeking support and building a strong support network.

Five KICKASS Questions to Reflect on:

1. How can you prioritize self-care and make time for activities that boost your mental well-being?

2. What are some mindfulness techniques you can incorporate into your daily routine to strengthen your mind-body connection?

3. Which stress-busting strategies resonate with you, and how can you implement them in your life?

4. How can you strengthen your support network and surround yourself with positive, uplifting people?

5. What are some ways you can cultivate a positive mindset and harness the power of positivity?

Now, take this KICKASS knowledge and put it into action! Nurturing your mental health is an essential part of living a life that kicks ass in every way possible. Embrace the journey, and remember – you've got this!

Chapter 18: The Power of Positivity

Section 1: The Optimism Advantage: How cultivating a positive mindset can enhance your life and happiness

Buckle up, my friends! We're about to embark on a wild ride exploring the boundless benefits of optimism. Get ready to shed those limiting beliefs and embrace the life-changing power of positivity. Let's dive in and make it KICKASS!

The Optimism Advantage: It's no secret that life can throw some pretty gnarly curveballs at you. But the way you respond to these challenges can mean the difference between living a life of happiness and success or succumbing to negativity and mediocrity. That's where the optimism advantage comes in. Having a positive mindset not only enhances your life but also boosts your happiness. So, let's explore how KICKASS optimism can be your secret weapon to conquering life's challenges.

The Science of Optimism: First things first, let's dive into the nitty-gritty. Studies have shown that optimists live longer, healthier, and happier lives compared to their pessimistic counterparts. But why? The answer lies in the biology of our brains. Optimism has been linked to lower cortisol levels (the stress hormone), better immune function, and a lower risk of developing chronic diseases. In short, optimism isn't just a feel-good philosophy – it's backed by solid science!

The Ripple Effect: Now, let's talk about the ripple effect. When you have a positive mindset, you're more likely to spread that optimism to others. Imagine the impact you can have on your friends, family, and coworkers just by being a beacon of positivity. The ripple effect of optimism is so powerful that it can transform entire communities, creating a KICKASS environment where everyone can thrive.

The Optimism-Happiness Connection: Here's the deal: happiness and optimism go hand in hand. When you cultivate a positive mindset, you're more likely to experience joy, satisfaction, and a higher quality of life. Optimists are better equipped to handle stress, bounce back from adversity, and maintain strong social connections. So, when it comes to living a KICKASS life, optimism is the key ingredient in the happiness recipe.

The Grit Factor: One word — grit. Optimists have it in spades. Grit is the passion and perseverance to achieve long-term goals, and it's a major factor in success. When you're optimistic, you're more likely to push through obstacles, stay committed to your goals, and ultimately achieve success. So, if you want to be a KICKASS achiever, start by embracing the power of positivity.

How to Cultivate Optimism: Ready to harness the optimism advantage? Let's explore some actionable tips to get you started.

1. Practice gratitude: Every day, make a list of at least three things you're grateful for. This simple exercise can help you shift your focus from what's wrong in your life to what's going right.

2. Surround yourself with positive influences: As the saying goes, "You are the average of the five people you spend the most time with." So, make sure your circle is filled with KICKASS optimists who lift you up and inspire you.

3. Find the silver lining: When faced with adversity, try to find the positive aspect or the lesson to be learned. This reframing technique can help you cultivate a more optimistic outlook on life.

4. Set realistic goals: Set achievable, yet challenging goals for yourself. When you experience success, your confidence and optimism will grow.

5. Develop a growth mindset: Embrace the belief that you can improve and grow through effort and perseverance. This mindset fuels optimism and encourages you to see challenges as opportunities to learn and grow.

6. Monitor your self-talk: Be mindful of your inner dialogue. Replace negative thoughts with positive affirmations to reinforce optimism and self-belief.

7. Practice self-compassion: Treat yourself with kindness and understanding, especially when you make mistakes or face setbacks. This will help you maintain a positive mindset and resilience in the face of challenges.

8. Engage in activities that bring joy: Make time for hobbies, interests, and activities that make you happy. This will strengthen your positive mindset and increase your overall well-being.

9. Build a support network: Establish and maintain strong relationships with people who encourage your optimism, offer guidance, and help you through tough times.

10. Embrace humor: Don't be afraid to laugh at yourself and find humor in difficult situations. This light-heartedness can help you keep a positive attitude and make challenges feel more manageable.

In conclusion, cultivating optimism is an essential ingredient for living a KICKASS life. It enhances your happiness, health, and success, while also having a positive impact on the people around you. By practicing gratitude, surrounding yourself with positive influences, and embracing a growth mindset, you can harness the optimism advantage and truly make your life extraordinary. Remember, the power of positivity is within your reach – all you have to do is grab it and make it KICKASS!

Section 2: Rewiring Your Brain: Techniques for fostering positive thinking and overcoming negative thought patterns

Are you ready to take control of your thoughts and rewire your brain for positivity? Hell yeah, you are! In this section, we'll explore some powerful techniques to help you foster positive thinking and crush those pesky negative thought patterns. Let's get started and make this journey KICKASS!

Neuroplasticity - The Science Behind Rewiring: Before we dive into the techniques, let's talk about the science behind rewiring your brain. It's called neuroplasticity – the brain's ability to change and adapt throughout your life. This means that, with the right strategies, you can literally rewire your brain to foster positive thinking and overcome negativity. Pretty KICKASS, huh?

Technique 1 - Mindfulness Meditation: Mindfulness meditation is a fantastic tool for rewiring your brain. It helps you become more aware of your thoughts and emotions, making it easier to recognize and replace negative thought patterns with positive ones. Start with just 10 minutes a day, and watch as your mindset shifts from doom and gloom to sunshine and rainbows.

Technique 2 - Cognitive Reframing: Cognitive reframing is a powerful technique that involves changing your perspective on a situation or event. By finding a more positive or constructive way to view a situation, you can rewire your brain to think more optimistically. Next time you face a challenge, ask yourself, "What's the silver lining?" or "What can I learn from this experience?"

Technique 3 - Positive Affirmations: Say it with me now: "I am KICKASS!" Positive affirmations are statements that reinforce your self-worth and optimism. Repeat them daily, and you'll create new neural pathways in your brain, making positivity your default setting.

Technique 4 - Visualization: Your brain is a powerful tool, and it doesn't know the difference between what's real and what's imagined. That's why visualization is so effective in rewiring your brain for positivity. Take a few minutes each day to visualize yourself achieving your goals, experiencing success, and living a happy, fulfilling life. This will help reprogram your brain for optimism and success.

Technique 5 - Journaling: Journaling is an excellent way to process your thoughts and emotions. By writing down your feelings, you can gain clarity on your thought patterns and actively work to replace negative thoughts with positive ones. Plus, it's a great opportunity to practice gratitude and remind yourself of all the KICKASS things in your life.

Technique 6 - Physical Activity: Exercise isn't just good for your body — it's also a powerful tool for rewiring your brain. Physical activity releases endorphins, those feel-good chemicals that boost your mood and combat negativity. So, get moving and make your brain KICKASS!

Technique 7 - Surround Yourself with Positivity: As we mentioned earlier, you're the average of the five people you spend the most time with. So, choose your tribe wisely. Surround yourself with positive, optimistic people who support and uplift you. Their energy will rub off on you, making it easier to rewire your brain for positivity.

In conclusion, rewiring your brain for positivity is a KICKASS way to overcome negative thought patterns and create a happier, more fulfilling life. With techniques like mindfulness meditation, cognitive reframing, and positive affirmations, you can take control of your thoughts and transform your mindset. Remember, you have the power to change your brain — and your life — for the better. Now go out there and make it KICKASS!

Section 3: The Law of Attraction: Harnessing the power of positivity to manifest your desires

KICKASS Intro: Prepare to have your mind blown, because we're about to dive into the amazing world of the Law of Attraction! This incredible phenomenon has the power to help you manifest your desires and create the KICKASS life you've always dreamed of. So, strap in and get ready to learn how to harness the power of positivity to turn your dreams into reality.

The Law of Attraction Unveiled: Alright, let's cut to the chase. The Law of Attraction (LOA) is the concept that like attracts like. In other words, positive thoughts and feelings attract positive experiences, while negative thoughts and feelings attract negative experiences. By focusing on your desires and maintaining a positive mindset, you can manifest those desires into your life. Sounds pretty KICKASS, right?

The Power of Visualization: One of the most potent tools in your LOA arsenal is visualization. When you vividly imagine your desires as if they've already been achieved, you're sending a powerful message to the universe that you're ready to receive them. So, put those daydreaming skills to good use and visualize your KICKASS life in all its glory!

The Importance of Belief: Here's the deal — belief is the cornerstone of the Law of Attraction. If you don't genuinely believe that you can achieve your desires, the universe won't deliver them to you. You need to have unwavering faith that your dreams are possible and that the universe is conspiring to make them a reality. So, embrace that KICKASS confidence and start believing in your ability to manifest your desires.

Taking Action: The Law of Attraction isn't just about positive thinking and visualization – it's also about taking action. After all, you can't just sit on your couch and expect your dreams to materialize out of thin air (though that would be pretty rad). You need to take KICKASS action towards your goals and trust that the universe will support your efforts.

The Art of Allowing: Sometimes, we can be our own worst enemies when it comes to manifesting our desires. We may have limiting beliefs or negative thoughts that block the flow of positivity and abundance. That's where the art of allowing comes in. To truly harness the power of the Law of Attraction, you need to let go of resistance and allow the universe to deliver your desires in its own perfect timing.

KICKASS Tips for Manifesting Your Desires:

1. Be crystal clear about your goals: The more specific you are about what you want to manifest, the easier it will be for the universe to deliver it to you.

2. Keep your vibrations high: Stay positive, practice gratitude, and engage in activities that bring you joy to maintain a high vibrational frequency that attracts abundance.

3. Use affirmations: Create powerful, positive statements that reinforce your belief in your ability to manifest your desires.

4. Stay patient and persistent: Remember that manifestation takes time, so be patient and keep taking KICKASS action towards your goals.

5. Trust the process: Have faith that the universe is working behind the scenes to bring your desires to fruition.

In conclusion, the Law of Attraction is an incredibly powerful tool that can help you manifest your desires and create a KICKASS life. By harnessing the power of positivity, embracing visualization and belief, taking action, and practicing the art of allowing, you can unlock the universe's abundance and make your dreams a reality. So, get out there and start manifesting like a KICKASS boss!

Section 4: Paying It Forward: Spreading positivity and kindness to create a happier, more connected world

Alright, folks, it's time to pay it forward! We've talked about the power of positivity and optimism, now let's discuss how we can share this KICKASS energy with others. Get ready to make a massive impact on the world and spread the love like there's no tomorrow. Let's make this world a better, happier place – together!

The Impact of Kindness: If there's one thing that can change the world for the better, it's kindness. Acts of kindness, big or small, can create a domino effect of positivity, leading to a happier and more connected society. When you share your positive energy with others, it not only benefits the recipient but also uplifts everyone around them, including yourself. So, if you want to create a KICKASS world, start by spreading kindness wherever you go.

The Art of Active Listening: One of the most powerful ways to spread positivity is through active listening. When you truly listen to someone, giving them your full attention and empathizing with their feelings, you're fostering a genuine connection that can make a lasting impact. In a world where people often feel unheard, the simple act of active listening can create a KICKASS difference in someone's life.

Random Acts of Kindness: Looking for a way to spread positivity and kindness? Try incorporating random acts of kindness into your daily routine. Whether it's complimenting a stranger, paying for someone's coffee, or helping an elderly person carry their groceries, these small gestures can make a huge difference in someone's day. The best part? The KICKASS feeling you'll get from brightening someone else's day will also boost your own happiness!

The Power of Connection: As human beings, we crave connection. Spreading positivity and kindness helps strengthen our connections with others, creating a sense of belonging and togetherness. When we feel connected to others, we're more likely to be happier, healthier, and more successful. So, if you want to create a KICKASS world, start by fostering connections and spreading love.

The Ripple Effect Revisited: Remember the ripple effect we talked about earlier? Well, it's back, and it's more important than ever. When you pay it forward by spreading positivity and kindness, you're not only making a difference in the lives of the people you directly impact but also inspiring others to do the same. This ripple effect can lead to a global movement of love, compassion, and understanding – creating a KICKASS world where everyone thrives.

KICKASS Strategies to Pay It Forward:

1. Start with yourself: Be kind to yourself and practice self-care. When you're filled with positivity and love, it's easier to spread it to others.

2. Express gratitude: Show appreciation for the people in your life by thanking them for their support and acknowledging their efforts.

3. Volunteer: Give back to your community by donating your time and energy to a local charity, non-profit, or social cause.

4. Encourage others: Offer words of encouragement and support to those who may be struggling or facing challenges.

5. Share your story: Share your journey of embracing positivity and kindness, inspiring others to do the same.

6. Smile: It's simple, but powerful. A genuine smile can brighten someone's day and spread positive vibes.

In conclusion, paying it forward by spreading positivity and kindness can create a happier, more connected world. By actively listening, engaging in random acts of kindness, and fostering connections, you can make a KICKASS impact on the lives of others and the world at large. Remember, you have the power to make a difference – so go out there and make it KICKASS! Keep paying it forward, share your positivity and kindness, and watch as the world transforms into a happier, more connected, and loving place. We're all in this together, so let's join forces and make our world the KICKASS place it deserves to be!

KICKASS Bonus Content:

Alright, folks, you asked for it – here's some extra KICKASS content to supercharge your journey of positivity and kindness. In this bonus section, you'll find additional tips, tricks, and resources to help you become the most positive, kind, and connected version of yourself. Get ready to dive in and make a KICKASS impact on the world!

1. Create a Positivity Playlist: Music can have a powerful effect on our emotions. Curate a playlist of your favorite uplifting, feel-good tunes that you can listen to whenever you need a boost of positivity.

2. Keep a Kindness Journal: Document your acts of kindness and the ways you've paid it forward. This

journal will serve as a reminder of the positive impact you're making and will inspire you to continue spreading love and positivity.

3. Join a Positivity Group: Connect with like-minded people who share your passion for positivity and kindness. This could be a local meetup group, an online community, or even a group of friends who support each other in their journey to create a happier world.

4. Challenge Yourself: Set a goal to perform a specific number of random acts of kindness each week or month. This challenge will keep you focused on spreading positivity and can create a fun and rewarding experience.

5. Read and Watch Inspiring Content: Seek out books, podcasts, documentaries, and films that inspire positivity and kindness. These resources can provide valuable insights, stories, and strategies to help you on your journey.

Chapter 18 Summary:

In Chapter 18, we explored the power of positivity and its incredible impact on our lives. We discussed the optimism advantage, rewiring your brain for positive thinking, the Law of Attraction, and paying it forward. By cultivating a positive mindset, harnessing the power of optimism, and spreading kindness, we can create a happier, more connected world. With the KICKASS strategies and bonus content provided in this chapter, you're now equipped to make a powerful, lasting impact on your life and the lives of those around you.

Five KICKASS Questions to Reflect on:

1. What is one area of your life where you could benefit from a more optimistic mindset?

2. Which rewiring technique from the chapter do you think would be most effective for you in overcoming negative thought patterns?

3. How can you apply the Law of Attraction to manifest a specific desire in your life?

4. What is one random act of kindness you can commit today to pay it forward and spread positivity?

5. How can you incorporate the KICKASS bonus content into your daily routine to further enhance your journey of positivity and kindness?

Chapter 19: The Art of Effective Communication

Section 1: The Power of Active Listening: Developing the skills to truly hear and understand others

You know what's KICKASS? Being a communication ninja. You want to know the first step to becoming one? Active listening. Buckle up, because I'm about to dive into the world of kickass active listening techniques that will transform the way you interact with people.

Let's start with a quote from the legendary Larry King: "I remind myself every morning: Nothing I say this day will teach me anything. So if I'm going to learn, I must do it by listening."

Active listening is the key to unlocking deeper understanding and connection with others. It's like a superpower, allowing you to truly hear and empathize with people, even when they're not saying much. This skill will help you build meaningful relationships, boost your career, and make you an all-around KICKASS person.

But how do you become a kickass active listener? Here are some steps to get you started:

1. Eliminate distractions: The first rule of active listening is to give the speaker your undivided attention. Put away your phone, close your laptop, and make eye contact. Be present in the conversation and show the speaker that they matter.

2. Show that you're listening: Give the speaker verbal and nonverbal cues that you're engaged. Nod your head, maintain eye contact, and offer short verbal affirmations like "Uh-huh" or "I see." This not only encourages the speaker but also helps you stay focused on what they're saying.

3. Don't interrupt: Let the speaker finish their thoughts before you jump in with your own. Interrupting is not only disrespectful, but it also prevents you from fully understanding their perspective.

4. Ask open-ended questions: When the time is right, ask questions that encourage the speaker to elaborate and share more. Avoid questions that can be answered with a simple "yes" or "no." Instead, use phrases like "Tell me more about..." or "What was your experience like when...?"

5. Reflect and clarify: As an active listener, it's your job to make sure you've understood the speaker correctly. Summarize their main points and ask for clarification if needed. This shows that you're engaged and genuinely interested in their perspective.

6. Don't impose your solutions: Avoid the temptation to jump in with your own solutions or advice. Instead, give the speaker space to explore their thoughts and feelings. Sometimes, the best way to help someone is simply to listen.

Now that you've got the basics down, it's time for a KICKASS exercise to help you practice your active listening skills.

Exercise: The next time you're in a conversation, try the "10-second rule." After the speaker finishes a sentence, count to 10 in your head before responding. This forces you to pause and reflect on what they've said, giving you the chance to process their words and ensure you've understood them correctly.

Remember, active listening is a skill that takes time and practice to develop. But once you've mastered it, you'll be well on your way to becoming a communication ninja, able to build deeper connections and navigate any conversation with ease.

When you're ready continue on to the next section, where we'll explore the gift of empathy and how it can revolutionize your communication game. Until then, keep practicing and stay KICKASS!

Section 2: The Gift of Empathy: Building deeper connections through compassionate communication

You know what's even more KICKASS than active listening? Empathy. It's like the cherry on top of the communication sundae. When you combine active listening with empathy, you become an unstoppable force, able to forge deep connections and understand others on a level that most people can only dream of.

The legendary Maya Angelou once said, "I've learned that people will forget what you said, people will forget what you did, but people will never forget how you made them feel."

Empathy is all about making people feel understood and valued.

So, how do you harness the power of empathy in your communication? Here are some KICKASS tips to get you started:

1. Put yourself in their shoes: When you're speaking with someone, try to imagine what it's like to be them. Consider their emotions, thoughts, and experiences. This will help you better understand their perspective and respond in a compassionate way.

2. Validate their feelings: Acknowledge the emotions the speaker is expressing, even if you don't agree with their perspective. Phrases like "I can understand why you feel that way" or "It sounds like that was really difficult for you" can go a long way in building trust and rapport.

3. Be curious: Ask questions to learn more about the speaker's feelings, thoughts, and experiences. Show genuine interest in understanding their perspective, and avoid making assumptions or judgments.

4. Offer support: When appropriate, offer your support and encouragement. Sometimes, a simple "I'm here for you" can make all the difference in the world.

5. Practice self-awareness: Be aware of your own emotions and reactions during the conversation. This can help you stay present and focused on the speaker, rather than getting caught up in your own feelings.

Ready for a KICKASS empathy exercise? Let's go!

Exercise: The next time you're in a conversation, try the "Three W's" technique. After the speaker shares their thoughts or feelings, respond with one of the following phrases:

- "What was that like for you?"
- "Why do you think that happened?"
- "When did you first start feeling this way?"

These questions encourage the speaker to dive deeper into their emotions and experiences, giving you a better understanding of their perspective.

By mastering the art of empathy, you'll become an incredible communicator who can build deep, meaningful connections with others. And that, my friend, is truly KICKASS.

Now you're ready for Section 3: Assertiveness Unleashed, where we'll explore how to balance confidence and respect in your communication style. Stay tuned and keep being KICKASS!

Section 3: Assertiveness Unleashed: Balancing confidence and respect in your communication style

Alright, it's time to dive into the world of KICKASS assertiveness. This section is all about finding that sweet spot between confidence and respect when communicating with others. I'm going to share some powerful strategies that will help you unleash your inner assertiveness while maintaining genuine connections with the people around you.

Let's kick things off with a quote from the badass Bruce Lee: "The successful warrior is the average person, with laser-like focus."

Ready to channel your inner warrior? Let's get started.

1. Know your worth: The first step towards becoming assertive is recognizing your own value. Understand that your opinions, needs, and desires are just as important as anyone else's. You deserve to be heard and respected, so own it!

2. Be clear and concise: When expressing your thoughts or needs, be direct and to the point. Use "I" statements to communicate your perspective without blaming or attacking the other person. For example, instead of saying "You're always late," try "I feel stressed when we're running late for appointments."

3. Stay calm and composed: Even in heated situations, keep your cool. Take deep breaths and focus on maintaining a steady, confident tone. By staying calm, you demonstrate self-control and earn the respect of those around you.

4. Listen and acknowledge: Just like we discussed in the active listening section, it's essential to listen to the other person's perspective and acknowledge their

feelings. This shows that you respect their opinion, even if you don't agree with it.

5. Stand your ground: Don't let others walk all over you. If someone tries to manipulate or guilt-trip you, stand firm in your beliefs and assert your boundaries. Remember, it's okay to say "no" when necessary.

6. Practice empathy: Understand that assertiveness isn't about winning or dominating; it's about finding a balance between your needs and the needs of others. Be empathetic to the feelings and perspectives of those around you, and strive to find common ground.

Now, for a KICKASS exercise to help you practice assertiveness:

Exercise: Choose a situation where you've been hesitant to assert yourself. Write down the reasons why you held back and how you would handle the situation differently using the strategies outlined above. Next, find a friend or family member to role-play the situation with you. This will help you gain confidence in asserting yourself in real-life scenarios.

There you have it! By incorporating these KICKASS assertiveness strategies into your communication toolbox, you'll be on your way to striking the perfect balance between confidence and respect. Keep practicing, stay focused, and remember – you've got this!

Next up, we'll tackle conflict resolution and how to navigate disagreements like a pro. Keep being KICKASS!

Section 4: Conflict Resolution: Strategies for navigating disagreements and finding common ground

KICKASS individuals know that conflict is inevitable, but they also know how to handle it like a boss. So, let's dive into some kickass conflict resolution strategies that will turn you into a master of navigating disagreements and finding common ground.

As the wise man, Dale Carnegie, once said, "When dealing with people, remember you are not dealing with creatures of logic, but with creatures bristling with prejudice and motivated by pride and vanity." That's why it's essential to approach conflicts with a level head and an open mind.

Here are some KICKASS strategies to help you resolve conflicts like a pro:

1. Stay calm and composed: It's easy to get emotional in a heated argument, but losing your cool can escalate the situation. Take deep breaths, count to 10, or even step away for a moment to gather your thoughts. Approach the conflict with a clear mind and a commitment to finding a resolution.

2. Listen actively: Just like in the first section of this chapter, active listening is crucial in conflict resolution. Make sure you truly understand the other person's perspective before responding. This not only shows respect but also helps you find the underlying issues that need to be addressed.

3. Address the problem, not the person: Focus on the issue at hand and avoid personal attacks. Criticizing the person instead of the problem can make them defensive and less willing to collaborate on finding a solution.

4. Find common ground: Look for areas where you both agree and build on that foundation. Focusing on shared values or goals can help you see the conflict from a more unified perspective.

5. Be willing to compromise: Remember, conflict resolution isn't about "winning" or proving that you're right. It's about finding a solution that works for both parties. Be open to making concessions and finding middle ground.

6. Be solution-oriented: Instead of dwelling on the problem or past mistakes, focus on brainstorming potential solutions. This proactive approach can help shift the conversation from negative to positive and increase the chances of finding a resolution.

7. Follow up: After you've reached an agreement, make sure to follow up and ensure that both parties are satisfied with the outcome. This can help prevent future conflicts and strengthen your relationship.

Now, let's put these KICKASS strategies into practice with a quick exercise.

Exercise: Think of a recent conflict you've had with someone. Reflect on how you handled the situation and identify areas where you could have applied the strategies mentioned above. Next time you face a disagreement, remember these techniques and watch how effectively you can resolve conflicts.

With these kickass conflict resolution strategies in your arsenal, you'll be unstoppable in navigating disagreements and finding common ground. Keep practicing, and remember: a true kickass individual knows when to stand their ground and when to seek compromise.

Stay tuned for more KICKASS communication tips and techniques, and remember to always embrace your inner KICKASS!

KICKASS Bonus Content: The Power of Nonverbal Communication

A KICKASS communicator knows that words aren't the only way to convey a message. In fact, nonverbal cues play a huge role in how we connect with others. To truly master the art of effective communication, you need to be aware of your body language, facial expressions, and tone of voice.

Here are some KICKASS tips for mastering nonverbal communication:

1. Maintain eye contact: Making eye contact shows that you're engaged and interested in the conversation. It also helps build trust and rapport.

2. Use open body language: Avoid crossing your arms or legs, as this can come off as defensive or closed-off. Instead, adopt a more open posture to show that you're receptive and approachable.

3. Be mindful of your facial expressions: Your facial expressions can speak volumes about your emotions and thoughts. Practice being aware of your expressions and how they might be perceived by others.

4. Modulate your tone of voice: A monotone voice can be perceived as disinterested or even rude. Vary your tone and pitch to convey enthusiasm and sincerity.

5. Be aware of personal space: Respecting others' personal space is essential for building trust and maintaining comfortable interactions. Be mindful of how close you stand or sit to others and adjust accordingly.

KICKASS Chapter 19 Summary:

In this KICKASS chapter, we covered the art of effective communication, including:

1. The Power of Active Listening: Developing the skills to truly hear and understand others.

2. The Gift of Empathy: Building deeper connections through compassionate communication.

3. Assertiveness Unleashed: Balancing confidence and respect in your communication style.

4. Conflict Resolution: Strategies for navigating disagreements and finding common ground.

Five KICKASS Questions to Reflect on:

Now, let's test your knowledge with these Five KICKASS Questions to Reflect on::

1. What is the first rule of active listening?
2. Why is empathy important in effective communication?
3. How can you balance confidence and respect in your communication style?
4. Name one strategy for navigating disagreements and finding common ground.
5. What is one tip for mastering nonverbal communication?

Take a moment to answer these questions and reflect on the KICKASS content you've just learned. Keep practicing and embracing your inner KICKASS, and watch as your communication skills soar to new heights!

Chapter 20: Crafting Your Life's Masterpiece

Congratulations! You've made it to the final chapter of this kickass journey. In this chapter, we'll explore how to craft your life's masterpiece by setting clear intentions, weaving together meaningful experiences, designing a legacy, and embracing the journey of life. So, let's dive in and make this chapter the most kickass yet!

Section 1: The Power of Intention: Setting a clear vision for the life you want to create.

KICKASS INTENTION: UNLOCK THE FULL POTENTIAL OF YOUR LIFE

We've come a long way, my friends, and I want to thank you for joining me on this KICKASS journey. Now, it's time to wrap it all up and make sure that you're fully equipped to create a life that will be remembered as a freaking masterpiece.

Intention is everything. If you want to create a KICKASS life, you need to start with a KICKASS intention. It's the force behind every great accomplishment, the driving power that pushes you to take massive action and achieve your wildest dreams.

So, let's dive in and discover the KICKASS power of intention and learn how to set a clear vision for the life you want to create.

A. CREATE A KICKASS VISION BOARD

Visualization is a powerful tool that can help you tap into the power of your intentions. A vision board is a visual representation of your goals, dreams, and the life you desire. To create a KICKASS vision board, follow these steps:

1. Get clear on your intentions: Write down your dreams and goals, focusing on the specific outcomes you want to achieve.

2. Gather images that represent your intentions: Look for pictures that inspire you and resonate with the life you want to create.

3. Assemble your vision board: Arrange the images on a large poster board or a digital platform like Pinterest, and place it somewhere you'll see it every day.

4. Take time to visualize: Spend a few minutes each day looking at your vision board and imagining yourself living the life you've created.

Remember, "A dream without a plan is just a wish." – Antoine de Saint-Exupéry

B. SET KICKASS GOALS

To harness the power of intention, you need to set KICKASS goals that align with your vision. Consider the SMART framework when setting your goals:

1. Specific: Clearly define what you want to achieve.

2. Measurable: Determine how you'll track your progress.

3. Attainable: Make sure your goals are realistic and achievable.
4. Relevant: Ensure your goals align with your overall vision.
5. Time-bound: Set a deadline for when you want to achieve your goals.

C. CREATE A KICKASS ACTION PLAN

Once you've set your goals, create an action plan to make them a reality. Break down your goals into smaller steps and assign a timeframe for each one. Remember, "The journey of a thousand miles begins with a single step." – Lao Tzu

D. EMBRACE KICKASS HABITS

Your daily habits will determine your success. Embrace habits that support your goals and vision, and ditch those that hold you back. As Aristotle once said, "We are what we repeatedly do. Excellence, then, is not an act, but a habit."

E. STAY ACCOUNTABLE TO YOUR KICKASS SELF

Accountability is key to staying on track with your intentions. Share your goals with a trusted friend or family member, or find an accountability partner who shares similar goals. Regularly check in with your progress and adjust your action plan as needed.

In conclusion, setting a clear vision for your life and harnessing the power of intention is the first step in crafting your life's masterpiece. Remember to create a KICKASS vision board, set KICKASS goals, create a KICKASS action plan, embrace KICKASS habits, and stay accountable to your KICKASS self.

Section 2: The Mosaic of Experiences: Weaving together a rich tapestry of meaningful moments.

KICKASS MOSAIC: CREATING A LIFE WORTH LIVING

Our lives are like a beautiful mosaic, composed of an intricate arrangement of experiences, memories, and emotions. To create a KICKASS life, we must weave together a rich tapestry of meaningful moments that will not only bring us joy and fulfillment but also leave a lasting impact on those around us.

So, let's explore how you can intentionally create a life that's a true work of art, full of KICKASS experiences that make every day worth living.

A. DISCOVER YOUR KICKASS PASSIONS

Finding your passions is key to creating a life filled with purpose and excitement. Take the time to explore what truly lights your fire and makes your heart sing. Remember, "Passion is energy. Feel the power that comes from focusing on what excites you." – Oprah Winfrey

B. CREATE KICKASS CONNECTIONS

Meaningful relationships are the cornerstone of a fulfilling life. Surround yourself with people who inspire, support, and uplift you. Seek out opportunities to connect with others and build strong bonds. As the saying goes, "Your vibe attracts your tribe."

C. EMBRACE KICKASS ADVENTURES

Life is too short to play it safe. Seek out new experiences and challenge yourself to step out of your comfort zone. Travel, take risks, and embrace the unknown. Remember, "Life begins at the end of your comfort zone." – Neale Donald Walsch

D. CULTIVATE KICKASS GRATITUDE

Gratitude is the key to unlocking happiness and contentment in your life. Make it a daily practice to express gratitude for the experiences, people, and moments that make your life extraordinary. As Tony Robbins says, "When you are grateful, fear disappears, and abundance appears."

E. CONTRIBUTE TO A KICKASS WORLD

To truly create a life that's a masterpiece, strive to leave the world a better place than you found it. Find ways to give back, help others, and create a positive impact. As Mahatma Gandhi famously said, "Be the change you wish to see in the world."

In conclusion, weaving together a rich tapestry of meaningful moments is essential for crafting your life's masterpiece. Discover your KICKASS passions, create KICKASS connections, embrace KICKASS adventures, cultivate KICKASS gratitude, and contribute to a KICKASS world.

Your life is a beautiful mosaic, and every experience is a unique piece that adds depth, texture, and color to your story.

Embrace the journey, my friend, and never forget: the more KICKASS moments you create, the more breathtaking your life's masterpiece will become.

Section 3: The Legacy Blueprint: Designing a life that leaves a lasting impact on the world.

KICKASS LEGACY: UNLEASH YOUR INNER PHILANTHROPIST

As our KICKASS journey together comes to a close, let's focus on a crucial aspect of crafting your life's masterpiece: your legacy. After all, what's the point of creating a KICKASS life if you don't leave a lasting impact on the world?

In this section, we'll explore the Legacy Blueprint, a roadmap to designing a life that not only benefits you but also positively impacts those around you and future generations. Let's dive in and make this part KICKASS!

A. IDENTIFY YOUR KICKASS VALUES

The foundation of your legacy lies in your core values. These values shape your actions, decisions, and the impact you'll leave behind. Reflect on what's most important to you and how you want to be remembered. Remember, "Your core values are the deeply held beliefs that authentically describe your soul." – John C. Maxwell

B. DEFINE YOUR KICKASS MISSION

With your values in mind, define your mission – the overarching purpose that guides your life. This mission should reflect the change you want to see in the world and how you'll contribute to it. As Mary Oliver once said, "Tell me, what is it you plan to do with your one wild and precious life?"

C. BUILD A KICKASS COMMUNITY

Your legacy is not just about what you do; it's also about the people you inspire and empower along the way. Surround yourself with like-minded individuals who share your values and mission, and together, create a community that supports and amplifies your impact.

D. GIVE BACK WITH KICKASS INTENT

Philanthropy and giving back are crucial components of a lasting legacy. Find causes that align with your values and mission, and support them through donations, volunteering, or advocacy. Remember, "The meaning of life is to find your gift. The purpose of life is to give it away." – Pablo Picasso

E. SHARE YOUR KICKASS WISDOM

Pass on your knowledge and experience to future generations. Whether it's through mentoring, teaching, writing, or speaking, sharing your wisdom can inspire others to create their own KICKASS legacies.

F. MEASURE YOUR KICKASS IMPACT

Continuously evaluate your impact on the world and make adjustments as needed. This will ensure your legacy remains true to your values and mission, leaving a lasting, positive mark on the world.

In conclusion, the Legacy Blueprint is your guide to designing a life that leaves a lasting impact on the world. Identify your KICKASS values, define your KICKASS mission, build a KICKASS community, give back with KICKASS intent, share your KICKASS wisdom, and measure your KICKASS impact.

Now, go forth and create a legacy that echoes through the ages, inspiring and uplifting those who come after you. It's time to leave your KICKASS mark on the world!

Section 4: The Final Chapter: Embracing the journey of life and finding joy in the pursuit of happiness, growth, and adventure.

KICKASS FINALE: CHERISH THE RIDE AND THRIVE ON THE ADVENTURE

As we reach the final moments of this KICKASS book, it's time to focus on the most important aspect of crafting your life's masterpiece — embracing the journey itself. Life is an incredible adventure, and it's essential to find joy in the pursuit of happiness, growth, and excitement.

A. KICKASS GRATITUDE: A GAME CHANGER

Gratitude is the secret sauce to living a KICKASS life. When you learn to appreciate the small victories, the moments of growth, and the lessons learned along the way, you unlock an unshakable sense of happiness and fulfillment. Make it a habit to express gratitude daily, and watch your life transform before your eyes.

B. LEAN INTO THE KICKASS DISCOMFORT

Growth happens outside your comfort zone. Embrace the challenges, the setbacks, and the uncertainty that comes with chasing your dreams. Remember, "Life begins at the end of your comfort zone." — Neale Donald Walsch

C. CELEBRATE KICKASS MILESTONES

Take the time to celebrate your achievements, no matter how big or small. Every milestone is a testament to your hard work, determination, and KICKASS attitude. As you progress on your journey, these moments of celebration will fuel your motivation to keep pushing forward.

D. BUILD A KICKASS TRIBE

Surround yourself with like-minded individuals who support, encourage, and inspire you. Your tribe should be a source of strength and camaraderie, pushing you to reach new heights and live your most KICKASS life.

E. NEVER STOP KICKASS LEARNING

The journey of life is a continuous process of learning, growing, and evolving. Stay curious, keep an open mind, and never stop seeking knowledge. As you learn, you'll become more resilient, adaptable, and capable of tackling any challenge that comes your way.

F. EMBRACE KICKASS IMPERFECTION

Perfection is an illusion. Embrace the imperfections in yourself and your journey, as they are what make you unique and human. It's through our flaws and mistakes that we learn and grow. Remember, "Imperfection is beauty, madness is genius, and it's better to be absolutely ridiculous than absolutely boring." – Marilyn Monroe

As we close this KICKASS book, I want to remind you that your life is a magnificent work in progress. Embrace the journey, cherish every moment, and find joy in the pursuit of happiness, growth, and adventure. You are the master of your own destiny, and the world is waiting for you to leave your indelible mark.

Thank you for embarking on this KICKASS journey with me. I have no doubt that you have the power to create an extraordinary life that will be remembered as a true masterpiece. Stay KICKASS, stay hungry, and never stop reaching for the stars.

Now, go out there and live your KICKASS life and remember Do Good, Live Life, Be Happy!

KICKASS BONUS CONTENT: Unleash Your Inner Warrior

Before we bid farewell, I've got some KICKASS bonus content to help you unleash your inner warrior and make the most of your life's journey. Remember, your life is a masterpiece, and it's up to you to make it a truly memorable and epic adventure.

BONUS 1: KICKASS MINDFULNESS EXERCISES

Practicing mindfulness can help you stay present, focused, and grounded on your journey. Try these KICKASS exercises to boost your mental strength and resilience:

1. KICKASS Breathing: Take deep, slow breaths, focusing on the sensation of your breath as it fills your lungs and then leaves your body. This simple practice can help you clear your mind and find inner peace.

2. KICKASS Body Scan: Focus on each part of your body, starting with your toes and working your way up to your head. As you do this, notice any tension, discomfort, or sensations and allow them to release.

3. KICKASS Loving-Kindness Meditation: Silently repeat phrases like "May I be happy, may I be healthy, may I be safe, may I be at ease" while focusing on yourself and then extending these wishes to others.

BONUS 2: KICKASS QUOTE COLLECTION

Surround yourself with inspiration by collecting and displaying your favorite KICKASS quotes. These powerful words can serve as a reminder of your purpose and motivation, pushing you to stay focused and committed to your goals.

BONUS 3: KICKASS PLAYLIST

Music can be a powerful motivator and mood booster. Create a KICKASS playlist filled with songs that inspire, energize, and empower you. Listen to it whenever you need a little extra motivation to tackle your goals and chase your dreams.

Summary of Chapter 20: Crafting Your Life's Masterpiece

1. The Power of Intention: Set a clear vision for the life you want to create by harnessing the power of intention, creating a KICKASS vision board, and setting KICKASS goals.

2. The Mosaic of Experiences: Weave together a rich tapestry of meaningful moments by embracing gratitude, leaning into discomfort, celebrating milestones, building a KICKASS tribe, and never stopping learning.

3. The Legacy Blueprint: Design a life that leaves a lasting impact on the world by embracing imperfection and focusing on your unique strengths and passions.

4. The Final Chapter: Embrace the journey of life by finding joy in the pursuit of happiness, growth, and adventure. Stay KICKASS, stay hungry, and never stop reaching for the stars.

FIVE KICKASS QUESTIONS TO REFLECT ON: TO PONDER:

1. What are your top three KICKASS intentions for your life's masterpiece?

2. How can you cultivate gratitude and celebrate your milestones on a regular basis?

3. What does your ideal KICKASS tribe look like, and how can you start building it today?

4. How can you embrace discomfort and use it as a catalyst for growth and transformation?

5. In what areas of your life can you practice KICKASS mindfulness to stay present and focused?

Remember, the end of this book is just the beginning of your KICKASS journey. Thank you for joining me on this wild ride, and I can't wait to see the incredible masterpiece you create. Stay KICKASS, my friends!

Message from Mickey

Wow, what an incredible journey it has been, you're a badass! You've made it to the end of this kickass book, and let's just say you're about to embark on a life-changing journey. You've learned how to embrace your true self, the power of saying "no," building meaningful relationships, embracing change, daring to dream big, and nurturing your mental health. You've discovered the art of effective communication, crafting your life's masterpiece, and so much more.

This book has been designed to help you unleash your inner badass and live life on your own terms. It's about empowering you to create a life that is authentic, fulfilling, and joyful. It's about helping you realize your full potential and live your best life.

So, be the badass that I know you are, it's time to take everything you've learned and put it into action. It's time to start living life on your own terms, embracing your passions, building meaningful relationships, and creating a life that brings you joy and fulfillment.

As you move forward on this journey, remember that life is a constant work in progress. Embrace the journey, stay curious, stay open, and keep pushing yourself outside of your comfort zone. As Carl W. Buehner once said, "They may forget what you said, but they will never forget how you made them feel."

So, go out there and make a positive impact on the world. Embrace your inner badass, and let your light shine bright. You've got this!

And now, for some final badass questions to keep you going:

1. What is one thing you can do today to start living life on your own terms?

2. How can you prioritize self-care and nurture your mental health on a daily basis?

3. What is one dream that you've been holding back on pursuing, and how can you start taking steps towards making it a reality?

4. What are some boundaries that you can set to protect your time, energy, and overall well-being?

5. How can you spread positivity and kindness in your daily interactions with others?

Remember, you're a badass, you have everything you need within you to create a life that brings you joy, fulfillment, and success. Now, go out there and make it happen and as always Live Life, Do Good, Be Happy!

Mickey Trivett

LIVE LIFE, DO GOOD, BE HAPPY!

PS... My life's mission is to empower, motivate, and educate others to live their lives to the fullest, make a positive impact, and find true happiness! And guess what, I've got some extra badass content lined up just for you! Get ready to take your kickassery to the next level with my Kickass Exercises Cheat Sheet and other incredible resources on the following pages. Buckle up and get ready to slay your goals, because we're in this together on this epic KICKASS JOURNEY!

Kickass Exercise Quick Cheat Sheet

Alright, let's do this! Get ready to unleash your inner badass with these kickass exercises that will help you craft your own masterpiece of a life! Each chapter of this book is packed with unique exercises designed to empower you to embrace your true self, prioritize your needs, and live life unapologetically. So get pumped, grab a pen and paper, and let's dive in!

Chapter 1: Embracing Your Badass Self

- *Write down three ways you can embrace your inner badass today and act on them.*
- *Create a "F*ck the Expectations" playlist with songs that inspire you to live life on your terms.*
- *Make a list of your quirks and unique qualities, and celebrate them with a mini dance party.*

Chapter 2: The Life-Changing Magic of Saying "No"

- *Say "no" to something that doesn't serve you today and feel the power of prioritizing your needs.*
- *Write down three personal boundaries you want to set and practice enforcing them in real-life situations.*
- *Create a "No-F*cks-Given" vision board with images that represent your priorities and goals.*

Chapter 3: Building Kickass Connections

- *Reach out to someone you admire and start a conversation. It can be as simple as a compliment or a question about their work.*

- *Schedule a virtual or in-person hangout with your inner circle and make it extra special by planning a kickass activity.*

- *Let go of a toxic relationship or situation that no longer serves you, and visualize the positive impact it will have on your life.*

Chapter 4: Embracing the Thrill of the Unknown

- *Try a new hobby or activity that scares you, like bungee jumping or public speaking.*

- *Embrace your failures by writing down one thing you've learned from each setback and how it's helped you grow.*

- *Go on an adventure, even if it's just exploring a new part of your city or trying a new food.*

Chapter 5: The Pursuit of Genuine Happiness

- *Start a gratitude journal and write down three things you're grateful for every day.*

- *Create a self-care plan and schedule in activities that bring you joy and peace.*

- *Perform a random act of kindness and see how it positively impacts both the recipient and yourself.*

Chapter 6: Fearlessly Facing Change

- *Write down three ways you've successfully navigated change in the past, and use them to inspire yourself to handle future changes with grace and resilience.*

- *Practice reframing negative thoughts into positive ones when facing a challenging situation.*

- *Celebrate your comebacks by creating a "Bounce Back" playlist with songs that motivate and inspire you.*

Chapter 7: Daring to Dream Big

- *Write down one audacious goal you want to achieve in the next year and create a roadmap to make it happen.*

- *Challenge your self-doubt by writing down three things you've accomplished that you're proud of and reflect on how they've contributed to your growth.*

- *Get inspired by watching a TED talk or reading a book about success stories that resonate with you.*

Chapter 8: Living Life, Doing Good, Being Happy (Mickey's Life Motto)

- *Create a "Live Life, Do Good, Be Happy" vision board with images that represent your ideal life.*

- *Volunteer or donate to a cause that aligns with your values and passions.*
- *Reflect on what kind of legacy you want to leave behind and write down actionable steps to make it happen.*

Chapter 9: Unleashing Your Inner Rebel

- *Take a different route to work or try a new restaurant, and reflect on how it feels to do something outside the norm.*
- *Break a societal norm that doesn't align with your values and reflect on how it's helped you be true to yourself.*
- *Use your creativity to express yourself through art, writing, music, or any other medium that speaks to you.*

Chapter 10: The Power of Vulnerability

- *Practice vulnerability by sharing something personal with someone you trust and seeing how it deepens your connection.*
- *Reflect on a time when you felt vulnerable but pushed through it to achieve something great. Write down how that experience helped you grow and what you learned from it.*
- *Practice being vulnerable in a low-stakes situation, like sharing a personal story with a stranger or trying a new activity with a group of people.*
- *Create a safe space for vulnerability by initiating a conversation with friends or family about a challenging topic and actively listening to their perspectives.*

Chapter 11: **Mastering Mindfulness**

- *Start a mindfulness practice, like meditation or yoga, and reflect on how it impacts your daily life.*
- *Practice mindful communication by fully listening to someone during a conversation and responding thoughtfully.*
- *Try a new mindfulness exercise, like a body scan or a mindful walk in nature.*

Chapter 12: **The Art of Letting Go**

- *Write a letter of forgiveness to someone who has hurt you, even if you don't send it.*
- *Declutter a physical space in your life and reflect on how it feels to have less physical and mental clutter.*
- *Practice surrendering control by letting go of a situation or outcome and accepting what happens.*

Chapter 13: **Building Bulletproof Confidence**

- *Write down three accomplishments you're proud of and reflect on how they contribute to your confidence.*
- *Take action towards a goal you've been putting off and feel the boost in confidence that comes from taking action.*
- *Embrace your charisma by practicing good posture, making eye contact, and speaking confidently in social situations.*

Chapter 14: **The Joy of Discomfort**

- *Reflect on a time when you stayed in your comfort zone and missed out on an opportunity. Write down what you learned from that experience and how you can challenge yourself in the future.*
- *Try something new that scares you, like a public speaking event or a solo travel adventure.*
- *Celebrate your resilience by writing down three challenges you've overcome and how they've made you stronger.*

Chapter 15: The Life-Changing Power of Habits

- *Choose one keystone habit, like exercise or journaling, and commit to practicing it every day for a week.*
- *Reflect on a negative habit you want to break and create a plan to replace it with a positive habit.*
- *Start small by implementing a tiny habit, like flossing one tooth or doing one push-up, and build on it gradually.*

Chapter 16: The Pursuit of Passion

- *Write down three passions you have and brainstorm ways to incorporate them into your daily life.*
- *Reflect on how pursuing your passions can positively impact your career, relationships, and overall happiness.*
- *Take action towards a passion project, like starting a blog or volunteering for a cause you care about.*

Chapter 17: Nurturing Your Mental Health

- *Reflect on the connection between your mental health and overall well-being, and identify one thing you can do to prioritize your mental health today.*
- *Practice self-compassion by giving yourself a break when you need it and speaking kindly to yourself.*
- *Implement a stress-busting strategy, like taking a walk in nature or practicing deep breathing exercises.*

Chapter 18: The Power of Positivity

- *Practice positive self-talk by reframing negative thoughts into positive ones.*
- *Use visualization techniques to imagine yourself achieving a goal or manifesting a desire.*
- *Perform a small act of kindness for someone, like buying a stranger a coffee or leaving a positive note in a public place.*

Chapter 19: The Art of Effective Communication

- *Practice active listening by fully engaging in a conversation with someone and reflecting on what you've learned.*
- *Put yourself in someone else's shoes and practice empathy by imagining their perspective on a situation.*
- *Stand up for yourself in a respectful and assertive way the next time you encounter a situation that challenges your boundaries.*

Chapter 20: Crafting Your Life's Masterpiece

- *Write down your intentions for the life you want to create and revisit them regularly to stay focused and motivated.*

- *Create a bucket list of experiences you want to have and start taking action towards making them a reality.*

- *Reflect on what kind of impact you want to have on the world and identify one way you can contribute to a greater good.*

Final Message from Mickey:

You are a badass. Yes, you! You have unique qualities that make you stand out in this world, and it's time to embrace them. It's time to prioritize your own needs and desires and live unapologetically. Don't let anyone dim your light or tell you that you're not good enough. You are worthy, and you deserve to live a kickass life.

Of course, living a kickass life doesn't mean it's all rainbows and unicorns. There will be setbacks and challenges along the way, but that's okay. Those are the opportunities for growth and learning. Don't give up when things get tough. Instead, practice self-compassion and resilience, and keep going. You have what it takes to overcome any obstacle that comes your way.

Remember, you are the master of your own life's masterpiece. You get to decide what goes in it, and how it's crafted. So, go ahead and paint outside the lines, take risks, and try new things. Be bold, be daring, be kickass.

Cheers to living life, doing good, and being happy - your kickass way!

Mickey Trivett

LIVE LIFE, DO GOOD, BE HAPPY!

KICKASS CONGRATULATIONS!

You've finished this book and kick-started your journey towards creating a life that's nothing short of a masterpiece. But don't forget, personal growth is an epic adventure that never truly ends. There's always more to learn, explore, and conquer. To keep the momentum going, we've put together a list of KICKASS resources that vibe with the themes of this book.

From books and podcasts that'll pump you up, to online communities and personal development programs tailored to your unique needs, these resources have your back as you continue to level up.

So, don't let this book be a one-hit-wonder. Let it be the spark that sets your soul ablaze with a desire to live life to the fullest, make a difference, and find true happiness. Dive into these KICKASS resources and keep growing, learning, and thriving as you sculpt your own awe-inspiring life's masterpiece.

KICKASS BOOKS:

1. "Daring Greatly" by Brené Brown - This book explores the power of vulnerability and encourages readers to embrace their imperfections as a path to greater connection and happiness.

2. "The Power of Now" by Eckhart Tolle - This book offers practical guidance on how to live in the present moment and overcome anxiety and negative thinking.

3. "Atomic Habits" by James Clear - This book provides actionable advice on how to create and maintain positive habits that can lead to lasting change.

4. "The Four Agreements" by Don Miguel Ruiz - This book offers a simple but profound guide to personal freedom based on four principles: be impeccable with your word, don't take anything personally, don't make assumptions, and always do your best.

5. "Big Magic" by Elizabeth Gilbert - This book encourages readers to tap into their creativity and pursue their passions without fear or self-doubt.

6. "The Gifts of Imperfection" by Brené Brown - a book about embracing imperfection and practicing self-compassion

7. "You Are a Badass" by Jen Sincero - a humorous and empowering guide to personal growth

KICKASS PODCAST:

1. "The School of Greatness" with Lewis Howes - This podcast features interviews with successful and inspiring people from various fields, exploring their journeys and the lessons they've learned.

2. "The Tim Ferriss Show" - This podcast delves into the habits and practices of successful people in business, sports, and entertainment, offering insights and strategies for personal growth.

3. "Happier" with Gretchen Rubin - This podcast offers practical advice on how to cultivate happiness and well-being in everyday life.

4. "The Marie Forleo Podcast" - This podcast features interviews with successful entrepreneurs and thought leaders, offering insights and strategies for personal and professional growth.

5. "Optimal Living Daily" - This podcast features narrated articles and blog posts on topics related to personal growth, mindfulness, and self-improvement.

6. "10% Happier" with Dan Harris - a podcast about mindfulness and meditation

7. "The Life Coach School" with Brooke Castillo - a podcast about mindset and personal growth

KICKASS WEBSITES:

1. Tiny Buddha - This website offers articles and resources on personal growth, mindfulness, and spirituality.

2. Mindful - This website provides resources and guidance on mindfulness meditation and how to incorporate mindfulness into everyday life.

3. Psychology Today - This website offers a wealth of articles and resources on mental health, personal growth, and relationships.

4. *TED Talks - This website features a vast library of talks on a wide range of topics, including personal growth and self-improvement.*

5. *Goodreads - This website provides a platform for readers to discover new books and connect with others who share their interests in personal growth and self-improvement.*

6. *Greater Good Magazine - A science-based magazine that explores the science of happiness, compassion, and social connection.*

7. *Zen Habits - A blog focused on simplifying life and cultivating mindfulness, offering practical tips and resources for personal growth.*

And there you have it, a KICKASS compilation of tools and resources to propel you forward on your personal growth odyssey and enable you to live your most KICKASS life. Embracing your one-of-a-kind traits and putting yourself first might seem daunting, but with the proper arsenal and backup, nothing is impossible. Remember, stumbling blocks and hurdles are merely stepping stones to growth, and by practicing self-compassion and resilience, you can conquer any obstacle in your path.

Now, it's time to get out there and show the world just how KICKASS you are! Harness these resources to keep crushing your personal growth journey and connect with the tribe and support system you need to flourish. You've totally got this!

Stay up-to date with Mickey by following him:

Social Platforms:

Facebook:

www.facebook.com/webcousa

Instagram:

https://www.instagram.com/mickeytrivett/

LinkedIn:

https://www.linkedin.com/in/mickeytrivett

Twitter:

https://twitter.com/mickeytrivett

On the Web:

Merchandise / Products

www.behappybrands.com

This Book

www.livelifedogoodbehappy.com

All Things Mickey

www.mickslife.com

For media questions or to contact Mickey directly, please email him at mickey@behappybrands.com

Made in the USA
Columbia, SC
13 October 2024